myrecipes

easy meal maker

myrecipes
easy
meal
maker

150 top-rated recipes • 500 delicious dinners

Oxmoor
House®

contents

A great dinner starts here!

How did you decide what to have for dinner last night? Be honest now. Did you build a meal around frozen pizza or whatever was left in the crisper? Did the idea hatch on your commute home or in the aisles of the grocery store? Was takeout involved?

Many roads lead to dinner, but on the busiest days it can be hard to know where to start. Even if you have a few go-to menus in your repertoire, a routine can quickly turn into a rut. And the "no-plan" plan may leave you eating a lot of unbalanced meals.

That's why we developed *MyRecipes Easy Meal Maker*, a cookbook that serves up **multiple menus with every top-rated dish.** No matter which recipe you turn to first—a main dish, a side dish, or even a dessert—you'll get inspired ideas for turning each recipe into a well-rounded meal. Hundreds of combinations help you keep things fresh.

This book includes **150 tried-and-true recipes, each approved by home cooks like you** and hand-picked from MyRecipes.com, the only website powered by Oxmoor House and America's favorite cooking magazines—*All You, Coastal Living, Cooking Light, Health, Real Simple, Southern Living,* and *Sunset.*

Whatever page you turn to first, the **Meal Maker beside each recipe gives you suggestions** for complementary dishes from elsewhere in the book and easy add-ons from the market. Chicken Kebabs and Nectarine Salsa—paired with the suggested grilled asparagus and Last-Minute Tropical Sherbet—makes a light and superfast weeknight dinner on the grill. Pork with Apples, Bacon, and Sauerkraut—served with garlic mashed potatoes and Caramel-Pecan-Pumpkin Bread Puddings—is perfect for a dinner party on a chilly evening.

Because every day's needs are a little different, we've labeled recipes to help you find just what you're looking for. **"Great for Company"** recipes make enough to please a crowd, **"Quick & Easy"** recipes can be prepared in less than 45 minutes, and **"Healthy Choice"** recipes offer lower-calorie, lower-fat options.

What's more, this book includes our **exclusive Scan-It/Save-It™ technology,** which lets you scan and save recipes to your smartphone for shopping lists and more. (See next page for complete details.) Each scan takes you to a digital version of the recipe on MyRecipes.com, where you can save the recipe to your online recipe folder. This handy innovation means you have access to your favorite dishes from the book even when you're away from home—like, say, at the grocery store, scratching your head about what's for dinner.

So stop stressing and start scanning these pages—knowing that you're on a path that leads directly to a delicious dinner.

The MyRecipes.com Editors

How to use the
Scan-It/Save-It™
digital features in this book

1. Download and open the Digimarc Discover app on your smartphone. It's free and available at the iTunes store for Apple devices and at the Google Play market for Android devices.

2. Position the phone 4 to 7 inches above any photo or box with a SCAN THIS label or icon (shown at right) as if you are about to take its picture. Use the phone's camera flash if necessary. If you have access to a Wi-Fi connection, downloads will be faster.

3. Hold the phone steady for a second or two. The app will click and buzz when it recognizes the image and then open the recipe right on your phone.

HOW IT WORKS

Invisible watermarks embedded in the page act as portals to bonus content. With the Digimarc Discover app, your phone recognizes the watermarks, opens the portals, and delivers the content.

WHAT'S SCANNABLE

Labels like these identify photos you can scan:

 SCAN THIS PHOTO to see and save the shopping list.

OR

WHAT SCANNING GETS YOU

- Each scannable photo in this book takes you to a digital version of the pictured recipe on MyRecipes.com, where you can save it to your personal recipe file.

- You can view the ingredients as a shopping list, add them to a longer list, and even see which ingredients are on sale at stores near you.

- You can also rate and review the recipe once you've given it a try.

REAL BUTTERMILK FRIED CHICKEN, *page 33*

SCAN THIS PHOTO to see and save the shopping list.

poultry

Bring new flavor and enjoyment to classic poultry dishes with these easy, affordable, and approachable dinnertime recipes.

meal maker

PICK A SIDE DISH

- Broccoli Slaw with Candied Pecans, page 158

OR

- arugula salad

ADD A DESSERT

- Last-Minute Tropical Sherbet, page 245

QUICK TIP

One whole roasted chicken yields about 3 cups of meat.

quick + easy

Avocado Chicken Salad

Makes 4 servings ▪ Prep: 20 minutes ▪ Total: 20 minutes

2 tablespoons olive oil
2 tablespoons fresh lime juice
⅜ teaspoon kosher salt
⅛ teaspoon freshly ground black pepper
2 cups shredded skinless, boneless rotisserie chicken breast

¼ cup chopped fresh cilantro
¾ cup refrigerated fresh salsa
1 ripe avocado, peeled and chopped
3 ounces tortilla chips

1. Combine first 4 ingredients in a medium bowl, stirring with a whisk. Add chicken and cilantro; toss to combine. Gently fold in salsa and avocado. Serve with chips.

For nutritional information on this recipe, please turn to the appendix on pages 248–251.

from CookingLight

great for company

Skillet Chicken Pot Pie

Makes 6 to 8 servings ▪ Prep: 30 minutes ▪ Total: 1 hour, 30 minutes

Chicken Pie Filling:
⅓ cup butter
⅓ cup all-purpose flour
1½ cups chicken broth
1½ cups milk
1½ teaspoons Creole seasoning
2 tablespoons butter
1 large sweet onion, diced
1 (8-ounce) package sliced fresh
  mushrooms

4 cups shredded cooked chicken
2 cups frozen cubed hash browns
1 cup matchstick carrots
1 cup frozen small sweet peas
⅓ cup chopped fresh parsley

Pastry Crust:
1 (14.1-ounce) package
  refrigerated piecrusts
1 egg white

1. Prepare Filling: Preheat oven to 350°. Melt ⅓ cup butter in a large saucepan over medium heat; add all-purpose flour, and cook, whisking constantly, 1 minute. Gradually add chicken broth and milk, and cook, whisking constantly, 6 to 7 minutes or until thickened and bubbly. Remove from heat, and stir in Creole seasoning.

2. Melt 2 tablespoons butter in a large Dutch oven over medium-high heat; add onion and mushrooms, and sauté 10 minutes or until tender. Stir in chicken, next 4 ingredients, and sauce.

3. Prepare Crust: Place 1 piecrust in a lightly greased 10-inch cast-iron skillet. Spoon chicken mixture over piecrust, and top with remaining piecrust, pressing to seal.

4. Whisk egg white until foamy; brush top of piecrust with egg white. Cut 4 to 5 slits in top of pie for steam to escape.

5. Bake at 350° for 1 hour to 1 hour and 5 minutes or until golden brown and bubbly.

from **SouthernLiving**

meal maker

PICK A SIDE DISH

- Balsamic Collard Greens, page 168

OR

- sliced tomatoes

ADD A DESSERT

- Luscious Lemon Bars, page 217

meal maker

PICK A SIDE DISH

- Grilled Corn Poblano Salad with Chipotle Vinaigrette, page 169

OR

- fruit salad

ADD A DESSERT

- Tart Lemon Ice with Crushed Strawberries, page 244

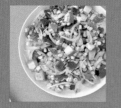

Chicken Enchiladas

Makes 4 servings ▪ Prep: 35 minutes ▪ Total: 55 minutes

5 tablespoons butter, divided
1 medium onion, chopped
1 medium-size red bell pepper, chopped
2 cups chopped cooked chicken
3 (4-ounce) cans diced green chiles, divided
3 cups (12 ounces) shredded colby-Jack cheese blend, divided

8 (8-inch) soft taco-size flour tortillas
2 tablespoons all-purpose flour
¾ cup chicken broth
½ cup milk
Toppings: fresh cilantro leaves, chopped tomato, shredded lettuce

1. Preheat oven to 350°. Melt 2 tablespoons butter in a large skillet over medium heat; add onion and bell pepper, and sauté 5 minutes or until tender.
2. Stir together onion mixture, chicken, 1 can diced green chiles, and 2 cups shredded cheese. Spoon a heaping one-third cup chicken mixture on 1 end of each tortilla, and roll up. Arrange enchiladas, seam sides down, in a lightly greased 13 x 9-inch baking dish.
3. Bake at 350° for 10 minutes.
4. Meanwhile, melt remaining 3 tablespoons butter in a heavy saucepan over low heat; whisk in flour until smooth. Cook, whisking constantly, 1 minute. Gradually whisk in chicken broth and milk; cook over medium heat, whisking constantly, 3 to 4 minutes or until thickened and bubbly. Remove from heat, and stir in remaining 2 cans green chiles.
5. Remove enchiladas from oven. Pour green chile mixture over enchiladas. Sprinkle with remaining 1 cup cheese.
6. Bake at 350° for 20 to 25 minutes or until bubbly. Serve with desired toppings.

from **Southern Living**

great for company

Chicken-and-Brisket Brunswick Stew

Makes 16 cups ▪ Prep: 25 minutes ▪ Total: 2 hours, 40 minutes

2 large onions, chopped
2 garlic cloves, minced
1 tablespoon vegetable oil
1½ tablespoons jarred beef soup base
2 pounds skinned and boned chicken breasts
1 (28-ounce) can fire-roasted crushed tomatoes
1 (12-ounce) package frozen white shoepeg or whole kernel corn
1 (10-ounce) package frozen cream-style corn, thawed
1 (9-ounce) package frozen baby lima beans
1 (12-ounce) bottle chili sauce
1 tablespoon brown sugar
1 tablespoon yellow mustard
1 tablespoon Worcestershire sauce
½ teaspoon coarsely ground pepper
1 pound chopped barbecued beef brisket (without sauce)
1 tablespoon fresh lemon juice
Hot sauce (optional)

1. Sauté onions and garlic in hot oil in a 7½-quart Dutch oven over medium-high heat 3 to 5 minutes or until tender.
2. Stir together beef soup base and 2 cups water, and add to Dutch oven. Stir in chicken and next 9 ingredients. Bring to a boil. Cover, reduce heat to low, and cook, stirring occasionally, 2 hours.
3. Uncover and shred chicken into large pieces using 2 forks. Stir in brisket and lemon juice. Cover and cook 10 minutes. Serve with hot sauce, if desired.
Note: We tested with Superior Touch Better Than Bouillon Beef Base and Muir Glen Organic Fire Roasted Crushed Tomatoes.

from **Southern Living**

meal maker

PICK A SIDE DISH

• Arugula Avocado Salad, page 154

OR

• corn tortilla chips

ADD A DESSERT

• Honeyed Apples with Ice Cream, page 223

meal maker

PICK A SIDE DISH

- New-Fashioned Apple and Raisin Slaw, page 184

OR

- cornbread sticks

ADD A DESSERT

- White and Dark Chocolate Pudding Parfaits, page 237

QUICK TIP

Don't drain the canned green chiles or navy beans before adding them to chili. The liquid in the cans adds extra flavor.

quick + easy

White Lightning Chicken Chili

Makes 11½ cups ▪ Prep: 30 minutes ▪ Total: 30 minutes

1 large sweet onion, diced
2 garlic cloves, minced
2 tablespoons olive oil
4 cups shredded cooked chicken
2 (14½-ounce) cans chicken broth
2 (4.5-ounce) cans chopped green chiles
1 (1.25-ounce) package white chicken chili seasoning mix
3 (16-ounce) cans navy beans
Avocado-Mango Salsa
Shredded Monterey Jack cheese
Fresh cilantro leaves

1. Sauté onion and garlic in hot oil in a large Dutch oven over medium-high heat 5 minutes or until onion is tender. Stir in chicken, next 3 ingredients, and 2 cans navy beans. Coarsely mash remaining can navy beans, and stir into chicken mixture. Bring to a boil, stirring often; cover, reduce heat to medium-low, and simmer, stirring occasionally, 10 minutes. Serve with desired toppings.
Note: We tested with McCormick White Chicken Chili Seasoning Mix.

Avocado-Mango Salsa

Makes about 2 cups ▪ Prep: 10 minutes ▪ Total: 10 minutes

1 large avocado, cubed
1 cup diced fresh mango
⅓ cup diced red onion
2 tablespoons chopped fresh cilantro
2 tablespoons fresh lime juice

1. Stir together avocado, mango, red onion, chopped fresh cilantro, and fresh lime juice.

from **Southern Living**

SCAN THIS PHOTO to see and save the shopping list.

meal maker

PICK A SIDE DISH

- Simple Sesame Salad, page 156

OR

- sliced cucumbers tossed in ginger dressing

ADD A DESSERT

- Key Lime Ice Cream Pie, page 243

quick + easy

Coconut-Curry Chicken Soup

Makes 7 servings ▪ Prep: 15 minutes ▪ Total: 25 minutes

4 cups water
3 cups fresh spinach leaves
½ pound snow peas, trimmed and cut in half crosswise
1 (5¾-ounce) package pad thai noodles (wide rice stick noodles)
1 tablespoon canola oil
¼ cup thinly sliced shallots
2 teaspoons red curry paste
1½ teaspoons curry powder
½ teaspoon ground turmeric
½ teaspoon ground coriander
2 garlic cloves, minced

6 cups fat-free, lower-sodium chicken broth
1 (13.5-ounce) can light coconut milk
2½ cups shredded cooked chicken breast (about 1 pound)
½ cup chopped green onions
2 tablespoons sugar
2 tablespoons fish sauce
½ cup chopped fresh cilantro
4 small hot red chiles, seeded and chopped, or ¼ teaspoon crushed red pepper
7 lime wedges

1. Bring 4 cups water to a boil in a large saucepan. Add spinach and peas to pan; cook for 30 seconds. Remove vegetables from pan with a slotted spoon; place in a large bowl. Add noodles to pan; cook 3 minutes. Drain; add noodles to spinach mixture in bowl.

2. Heat canola oil in pan over medium-high heat. Add shallots and next 5 ingredients (through garlic) to pan; sauté 1 minute, stirring constantly. Add chicken broth to pan, and bring to a boil. Add coconut milk to pan; reduce heat, and simmer 5 minutes. Add chicken, onions, sugar, and fish sauce to pan; cook for 2 minutes. Pour chicken mixture over noodle mixture in bowl. Stir in cilantro and chiles. Serve with lime wedges.

For nutritional information on this recipe, please turn to the appendix on pages 248–251.

from CookingLight

quick + easy

Lemon Chicken

Makes 8 servings ■ Prep: 10 minutes ■ Total: 30 minutes

4 skinned and boned chicken
    breasts (about 1½ pounds)
1 teaspoon salt
½ teaspoon pepper
⅓ cup all-purpose flour
4 tablespoons butter, divided
2 tablespoons olive oil, divided

¼ cup chicken broth
¼ cup lemon juice
8 lemon slices
¼ cup chopped fresh flat-leaf
    parsley
Garnish: lemon slices

1. Cut each chicken breast in half lengthwise. Place chicken between 2 sheets of heavy-duty plastic wrap; flatten to ¼-inch thickness, using a rolling pin or flat side of a meat mallet. Sprinkle chicken with salt and pepper. Lightly dredge chicken in flour, shaking off excess.

2. Melt 1 tablespoon butter with 1 tablespoon olive oil in a large nonstick skillet over medium-high heat. Cook half of chicken in skillet 2 to 3 minutes on each side or until golden brown and done. Transfer chicken to a serving platter, and keep warm. Repeat procedure with 1 tablespoon butter and remaining olive oil and chicken.

3. Add broth and lemon juice to skillet, and cook 1 to 2 minutes or until sauce is slightly thickened, stirring to loosen particles from bottom of skillet. Add 8 lemon slices.

4. Remove skillet from heat; add parsley and remaining 2 tablespoons butter, and stir until butter melts. Pour sauce over chicken. Serve immediately. Garnish, if desired.

from **Southern Living**

meal maker

PICK A SIDE DISH

- Rosemary Mashed Sweet Potatoes with Shallots, page 209

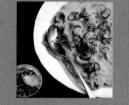

OR

- roasted green beans

ADD A DESSERT

- Mini Berry Cobblers, page 224

SCAN THIS PHOTO
to see and save
the shopping list.

healthy choice

Chicken Kebabs and Nectarine Salsa

Make 4 servings ▪ Prep: 10 minutes ▪ Total: 40 minutes

1 tablespoon brown sugar
1 tablespoon olive oil
1 tablespoon fresh lime juice
2 teaspoons chili powder
1 teaspoon bottled minced garlic
½ teaspoon kosher salt
½ teaspoon ground cumin
¼ teaspoon freshly ground black pepper
1½ pounds skinless, boneless chicken breast halves, cut into 24 (2-inch) pieces
1 large red onion, cut into 32 (2-inch) pieces

Cooking spray
2 cups diced nectarines (about 3)
½ cup diced red bell pepper
¼ cup thinly sliced red onion
2 tablespoons fresh cilantro leaves
1½ tablespoons fresh lime juice
2 teaspoons minced seeded jalapeño pepper
¼ teaspoon kosher salt
½ cup diced peeled avocado

1. Preheat broiler. Combine first 9 ingredients in a shallow dish; let stand 15 minutes.
2. Thread 4 onion pieces and 3 chicken pieces alternately onto each of 8 (12-inch) skewers. Place skewers on broiler pan coated with cooking spray. Broil 12 minutes or until chicken is done, turning occasionally.
3. Combine nectarines and next 6 ingredients (through ¼ teaspoon salt) in a bowl. Gently stir in avocado.

For nutritional information on this recipe, please turn to the appendix on pages 248–251.

from CookingLight

meal maker

PICK A SIDE DISH

• Herbed Couscous Pilaf, page 196

OR

• grilled asparagus

ADD A DESSERT

• Last-Minute Tropical Sherbet, page 245

meal maker

PICK A SIDE DISH

- Caramelized Spicy Green Beans, page 171

OR

- roasted Broccolini

ADD A DESSERT

- Key Lime Ice Cream Pie, page 243

QUICK TIP

Baguette that's a little stale is perfectly fine for the croutons in this salad.

healthy choice

Greek Chicken Bread Salad

Makes 4 servings ▪ Prep: 10 minutes ▪ Total: 45 minutes

3 ounces cubed French bread baguette, crust removed
Cooking spray
1 tablespoon chopped fresh oregano
3 tablespoons olive oil
1½ tablespoons red wine vinegar
2 teaspoons minced garlic
2 teaspoons grated lemon rind
⅛ teaspoon crushed red pepper
1 pound skinless, boneless chicken breast halves

¼ teaspoon freshly ground black pepper
⅛ teaspoon kosher salt
3 cups chopped romaine lettuce
1 cup sliced red bell pepper (about 1 large)
½ cup sliced pepperoncini peppers
1.5 ounces feta cheese, crumbled (about ⅓ cup)

1. Preheat broiler.
2. Place baguette cubes on a baking sheet; coat with cooking spray. Broil 2 minutes or until edges are browned, turning once.
3. Reduce oven temperature to 425°.
4. Combine oregano and next 5 ingredients (through crushed red pepper) in a large bowl, stirring with a whisk; set aside.
5. Heat a large ovenproof skillet over medium-high heat; coat pan with cooking spray. Sprinkle chicken evenly with black pepper and salt. Place chicken in pan; cook 4 minutes on each side or until browned. Place pan in oven, and bake at 425° for 10 minutes or until chicken is done. Remove pan from oven. Let chicken stand 5 minutes; slice thinly across the grain.
6. Add bread cubes, lettuce, bell pepper, pepperoncini peppers, and feta to bowl with oregano mixture; toss well. Place about 1⅓ cups salad on each of 4 plates. Top each serving with about 3 ounces chicken.

For nutritional information on this recipe, please turn to the appendix on pages 248–251.

from CookingLight

SCAN THIS PHOTO to see and save the shopping list.

healthy choice

Maple-Mustard Glazed Chicken

Makes 4 servings ▪ Prep: 15 minutes ▪ Total: 30 minutes

---

2 teaspoons olive oil
4 (6-ounce) skinless, boneless chicken breast halves
½ teaspoon freshly ground black pepper
¼ teaspoon salt
¼ cup fat-free, lower-sodium chicken broth

¼ cup maple syrup
2 teaspoons chopped fresh thyme
2 medium garlic cloves, thinly sliced
1 tablespoon cider vinegar
1 tablespoon stone-ground mustard

1. Preheat oven to 400°.
2. Heat a large ovenproof skillet over medium-high heat. Add oil; swirl to coat. Sprinkle chicken with pepper and salt. Add chicken to pan; sauté 2 minutes on each side or until browned. Remove chicken from pan. Add broth, syrup, thyme, and garlic to pan; bring to a boil, scraping pan to loosen browned bits. Cook 2 minutes, stirring frequently. Add vinegar and mustard; cook for 1 minute, stirring constantly. Return chicken to pan, and spoon mustard mixture over chicken. Bake at 400° for 10 minutes or until the chicken is done. Remove chicken from pan; let stand 5 minutes. Place pan over medium heat; cook mustard mixture 2 minutes or until liquid is syrupy, stirring frequently. Serve with chicken.

For nutritional information on this recipe, please turn to the appendix on pages 248–251.

from CookingLight

meal maker

PICK A SIDE DISH

- Buttery Lemon Broccolini, page 160

OR

- Caesar salad

ADD A DESSERT

- Grilled Pound Cake with Lemon Cream and Blueberries, page 232

healthy choice

Grilled Chicken Florentine Pasta

Makes 4 servings ▪ Prep: 10 minutes ▪ Total: 45 minutes

2 (6-ounce) bone-in chicken breasts, skinned
¾ teaspoon salt, divided
¾ teaspoon black pepper, divided
Cooking spray
8 ounces uncooked linguine
2 tablespoons canola oil
3 tablespoons all-purpose flour
1 teaspoon chopped fresh garlic
1 cup whole milk
1 cup fat-free, lower-sodium chicken broth
3 ounces Parmesan cheese, grated (about ¾ cup)
4 cups fresh spinach leaves

1. Preheat grill to medium-high heat.
2. Sprinkle chicken with ¼ teaspoon salt and ¼ teaspoon pepper. Place chicken on grill rack coated with cooking spray, and grill for 8 minutes on each side or until done. Let stand 10 minutes. Carve chicken off bones, and thinly slice.
3. Cook the pasta according to package directions. Drain well; keep warm.
4. Heat a large nonstick skillet over medium-high heat. Add oil to pan; swirl to coat. Add flour and garlic; cook until garlic is browned (about 2 minutes), stirring constantly. Add milk and broth, stirring with a whisk; bring to a simmer, and cook 2 minutes or until thickened. Add cheese, stirring until cheese melts. Add remaining ½ teaspoon salt, remaining ½ teaspoon pepper, and spinach; stir until spinach wilts. Add pasta and chicken; toss to combine.

For nutritional information on this recipe, please turn to the appendix on pages 248–251.

from CookingLight

SCAN THIS PHOTO
to see and save
the shopping list.

healthy choice

Quinoa Salad with Chicken, Avocado, and Oranges

Makes 4 to 6 servings ▪ Prep: 10 minutes ▪ Total: 40 minutes

1¼ cups quinoa
1 teaspoon chili powder
1 tablespoon minced garlic, divided
Zest of 1 lime
2 teaspoons plus 3 tablespoons olive oil
1 teaspoon kosher salt, divided
Pepper to taste, divided

1 pound boned, skinned chicken thighs
¼ cup lime juice
½ cup chopped fresh cilantro
4 large oranges, peeled and segmented
2 ripe avocados, peeled and cubed

1. Cook quinoa according to package directions and fluff with a fork. Transfer to a large bowl and let cool.

2. Preheat broiler with a rack set 4 to 6 inches from heat. In a large bowl, stir together chili powder, 2 teaspoons garlic, the lime zest, 2 teaspoons oil, and ½ teaspoon each salt and pepper. Add chicken and toss to coat. Put chicken on a baking sheet and broil, turning once, until browned and cooked through, about 12 minutes total. Let cool slightly, then slice and add to reserved quinoa.

3. Add remaining ingredients to quinoa and chicken; toss to coat.

For nutritional information on this recipe, please turn to the appendix on pages 248–251.

from **Sunset**

meal maker

PICK A SIDE DISH

- Curried Cauliflower with Capers, page 167

OR

- roasted butternut squash

ADD A DESSERT

- Free-form Strawberry Cheesecake, page 229

QUICK TIP

If you like quinoa, make a little extra to add to other salads throughout the week. (Quinoa triples when it cooks, so reserve 3¾ cups cooked quinoa for this recipe.)

- Lavender-Scented Summer Fruit Salad, page 183

OR

- potato chips

ADD A DESSERT

- Red Velvet Cupcakes, page 230

QUICK TIP

When cooking over high heat or grilling, opt for skinless boneless chicken thighs rather than breasts. They retain more moisture and flavor.

quick + easy

Grilled Chicken Sliders and Apricot Chutney Spread

Makes 4 servings ▪ Prep: 10 minutes ▪ Total: 20 minutes

½ teaspoon freshly ground black pepper
⅜ teaspoon ground red pepper
⅛ teaspoon salt
1½ pounds skinless, boneless chicken thighs
Cooking spray

3 apricots, halved and pitted
1 tablespoon water
1 tablespoon cider vinegar
1 tablespoon Dijon mustard
2 garlic cloves, chopped
8 (1.3-ounce) mini sandwich buns

1. Combine first 3 ingredients in a small bowl. Sprinkle chicken with pepper mixture. Place a large grill pan over medium-high heat; coat pan with cooking spray. Add chicken to pan; cook 5 minutes on each side or until done. Cool slightly; shred meat.
2. Recoat pan with cooking spray. Place apricots, cut sides down, on pan; cook 6 minutes over medium-high heat or until tender and lightly browned, turning after 4 minutes. Place apricots and next 4 ingredients (through garlic) in a food processor; process until smooth.
3. Spread about ½ teaspoon apricot chutney over cut side of each sandwich bun half. Place about ⅓ cup chicken on bottom bun; cover with top half of bun.

For nutritional information on this recipe, please turn to the appendix on pages 248–251.

from CookingLight

quick + easy

Spicy Basil Chicken

Makes 4 servings ▪ Prep: 5 minutes ▪ Total: 20 minutes

2 teaspoons canola oil
¼ cup minced shallots
3 garlic cloves, thinly sliced
6 (4-ounce) skinless, boneless chicken thighs, cut into 1-inch pieces
1 tablespoon fish sauce
2 teaspoons sugar

2 teaspoons lower-sodium soy sauce
1¼ teaspoons sambal oelek (ground fresh chile paste)
1 teaspoon water
½ teaspoon cornstarch
⅛ teaspoon salt
⅓ cup sliced basil leaves

1. Heat a large nonstick skillet over medium-high heat. Add oil to pan; swirl to coat. Add shallots and garlic to pan; cook for 30 seconds or until fragrant. Add chicken to pan; cook 13 minutes or until chicken is done. Combine fish sauce and next 6 ingredients (through salt) in a small bowl, stirring with a whisk. Add fish sauce mixture to pan, and cook for 1 minute or until mixture thickens, stirring to coat chicken. Remove from heat. Stir in basil.

For nutritional information on this recipe, please turn to the appendix on pages 248–251.

from CookingLight

meal maker

PICK A SIDE DISH

- Everyday Roast Vegetables, page 181

OR

- basmati rice

ADD A DESSERT

- Strawberry-Rhubarb Ice Cream, page 246

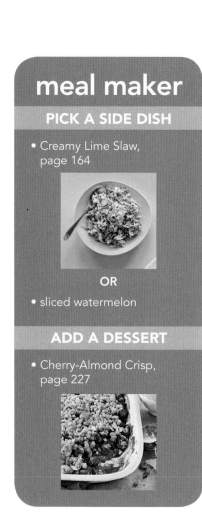

Chili-Lime Drumsticks

Makes 8 servings ▪ Prep: 5 minutes ▪ Total: 1 hour, 5 minutes

16 chicken drumsticks
Salt and pepper
¼ cup unsalted butter, melted
    and cooled

¼ cup fresh lime juice
1 tablespoon chili powder
1 clove garlic, chopped
1 teaspoon sugar

1. Preheat oven to 400°F. Rinse drumsticks, pat dry, and season with salt and pepper. Place in a flat layer in 2 large baking pans.
2. Mix remaining ingredients. Pour over drumsticks; turn them to coat. Cover with foil; bake 15 minutes. Remove foil, and turn drumsticks; bake until cooked through, 35 minutes, basting often with pan juices. Let rest for 10 minutes, then serve hot; or let cool, cover, and refrigerate to serve cold.

For nutritional information on this recipe, please turn to the appendix on pages 248–251.

from all*you*

great for company

Rosemary-Garlic Chicken Quarters

Makes 6 to 8 servings ■ Prep: 25 minutes ■ Total: 4 hours, 25 minutes

3 carrots or celery ribs
5 pounds chicken leg quarters
2 tablespoons chopped fresh rosemary
2 teaspoons pimentón (sweet smoked Spanish paprika)
2½ teaspoons kosher salt, divided

1¼ teaspoons freshly ground pepper, divided
12 garlic cloves, sliced
3 tablespoons olive oil
½ cup chicken broth
2 pounds fingerling Yukon gold potatoes, halved
1 teaspoon olive oil

1. Place carrots in a single layer in a 5-quart slow cooker.
2. Remove skin from chicken, and trim fat. Stir together rosemary, pimentón, 1½ teaspoons salt, and 1 teaspoon pepper. Rub mixture over chicken.
3. Sauté garlic in 3 tablespoons hot oil in a large skillet over medium heat 2 minutes or until golden brown. Transfer to a bowl using a slotted spoon; reserve oil in skillet. Cook half of chicken in reserved oil in skillet 3 to 4 minutes on each side or until deep golden brown. Transfer to slow cooker, reserving drippings in skillet. Repeat with remaining chicken.
4. Add broth and garlic to reserved drippings in skillet, and cook 1 minute, stirring to loosen particles from bottom of skillet; pour over chicken in slow cooker. Cover and cook on HIGH 2 hours.
5. Toss potatoes with 1 teaspoon oil and remaining 1 teaspoon salt and ¼ teaspoon pepper; add to slow cooker. Cover and cook 2 more hours.
6. Transfer chicken and potatoes to a serving platter, and pour juices from slow cooker through a fine wire-mesh strainer into a bowl; skim fat from juices. Serve immediately with chicken and potatoes.

from **Southern Living**

meal maker

PICK A SIDE DISH

• Steamed Carrots with Garlic-Ginger Butter, page 163

OR

• sautéed spinach

ADD A DESSERT

• Brown Sugar-Cinnamon Peach Pie, page 238

meal maker

PICK A SIDE DISH

- Garlic-Roasted Kale, page 174

OR

- brown rice

ADD A DESSERT

- Bittersweet Fudge with Sea Salt, page 222

QUICK TIP

If you can't find fresh herbs, you can use dried herbs. Just use one-third as much as the recipe calls for.

great for company

Chicken in Wine Sauce

Makes 6 servings ▪ Prep: 30 minutes ▪ Total: 1 hour, 15 minutes

4 bone-in chicken thighs, skinned
2 bone-in chicken breast halves, halved crosswise and skinned
½ teaspoon kosher salt, divided
½ teaspoon freshly ground black pepper, divided
2 teaspoons canola oil
1 cup chopped onion
½ cup thinly sliced carrot
½ cup thinly sliced celery
1 tablespoon minced fresh garlic
2 cups dry white wine
1 cup unsalted chicken stock

2 tablespoons all-purpose flour
3 tablespoons chopped fresh tarragon
3 tablespoons chopped fresh flat-leaf parsley, divided
1 tablespoon whole-grain Dijon mustard
1 bay leaf
1 tablespoon unsalted butter
2 cups cherry tomatoes
Cooking spray
2 slices applewood-smoked bacon, cooked and crumbled

1. Preheat oven to 325°.

2. Heat a Dutch oven over medium heat. Sprinkle chicken evenly with ¼ teaspoon salt and ¼ teaspoon pepper. Add oil to pan; swirl to coat. Add half of chicken to pan, flesh side down. Cook 4 minutes or until browned; remove from pan. Repeat with remaining chicken. Set chicken aside.

3. Add onion, carrot, celery, and garlic to pan; cook 6 minutes, stirring occasionally. Add wine; cook 2 minutes, scraping pan to loosen browned bits. Return chicken to pan, flesh side up. Combine stock and flour in a bowl, stirring with a whisk until smooth. Add stock mixture to pan.

4. Stir in tarragon, 2 tablespoons parsley, mustard, and bay leaf, and bring to a boil. Cover and bake at 325° for 45 minutes or until chicken is done and very tender. Remove pan from oven. Remove chicken from pan, and top with ¼ cup cooking liquid. Keep warm. Heat pan over medium-high heat, and bring to a boil. Boil 5 minutes or until mixture is reduced to 3 cups. Whisk in butter, remaining ¼ teaspoon salt, and remaining ¼ teaspoon pepper. Discard bay leaf.

5. Preheat broiler.

6. Arrange tomatoes in a single layer on a jelly-roll pan; lightly coat with cooking spray. Broil 6 minutes or until blistered. Sprinkle chicken with tomatoes, crumbled bacon, and remaining 1 tablespoon parsley. Serve with sauce.

For nutritional information on this recipe, please turn to the appendix on pages 248–251.

from CookingLight

SCAN THIS PHOTO to see and save the shopping list.

SCAN THIS PHOTO to see and save the shopping list.

great for company

Real Buttermilk Fried Chicken

Makes 6 to 8 servings ▪ Prep: 50 minutes ▪ Total: 2 hours, 50 minutes

1 (3½-pound) whole chicken, cut
    into 8 pieces
2 cups buttermilk
1 tablespoon Creole seasoning
1 teaspoon salt
¼ teaspoon freshly ground
    pepper

3 cups all-purpose flour
9 cups shortening
Garnishes: lemon wedges, fresh
    flat-leaf parsley

1. Place chicken in a large zip-top plastic freezer bag. Add buttermilk; seal and chill 2 hours.

2. Remove chicken from buttermilk, discarding buttermilk. Sprinkle chicken with Creole seasoning and next 2 ingredients. Place flour on a large plate or in a shallow dish. Dredge chicken in flour, shaking off excess.

3. Melt shortening to depth of 1½ inches in a Dutch oven or heavy-bottomed skillet at least 10 inches wide and 3 inches deep over medium-high heat; heat to 360°. Fry chicken, in batches, turning often, 15 to 20 minutes or until evenly browned and done. Drain on a wire rack over paper towels. Garnish, if desired.

from **Southern Living**

meal maker

PICK A SIDE DISH

- Balsamic Collard Greens,
  page 168

OR

- steamed corn on the cob

ADD A DESSERT

- Real Banana Pudding,
  page 235

meal maker

PICK A SIDE DISH

- Lemon-Garlic Swiss Chard, page 178

OR

- romaine salad and garlic bread

ADD A DESSERT

- So Good Brownies, page 220

QUICK TIP

No-boil noodles cut down on prep time and make this lasagna an ideal make-ahead dish. Assemble the lasagna in the morning, cover and refrigerate it, and bake just before dinner.

great for company

Turkey Sausage Lasagna

Makes 10 servings ■ Prep: 30 minutes ■ Total: 1 hour, 25 minutes

2 tablespoons olive oil
½ cup finely chopped onion
5 garlic cloves, minced
¼ teaspoon kosher salt
¼ teaspoon freshly ground black pepper
1 pound mild turkey Italian sausage
1 (28-ounce) can crushed tomatoes with basil
1 (14.5-ounce) can no-salt-added diced tomatoes with basil, garlic, and oregano

6 ounces shredded part-skim mozzarella cheese (about 1½ cups), divided
2 ounces grated fresh Parmesan cheese (about ½ cup)
1 (16-ounce) container 2% low-fat cottage cheese
2 large eggs, lightly beaten
Cooking spray
12 no-boil lasagna noodles

1. Preheat oven to 350°.
2. Heat a large skillet over medium-high heat. Add oil; swirl to coat. Add onion; cook 3 minutes, stirring occasionally. Add garlic, salt, and pepper; cook 1 minute. Remove casings from sausage. Add sausage to pan; cook 5 minutes or until browned, stirring to crumble. Add tomatoes. Bring to a boil; reduce heat, and simmer, uncovered, 10 minutes. Remove from heat.
3. While sauce simmers, combine 1 cup mozzarella cheese, Parmesan cheese, cottage cheese, and eggs.
4. Spoon ½ cup meat sauce into a 13 x 9–inch baking dish coated with cooking spray. Place 4 noodles over sauce. Spread half of cheese mixture over noodles; top with 2 cups sauce. Repeat procedure with 4 noodles, remaining half of cheese mixture, and 2 cups sauce. Top with remaining 4 noodles; spread remaining sauce over noodles. Sprinkle with remaining ½ cup mozzarella cheese.
5. Cover and bake at 350° for 40 minutes or until bubbly and noodles are tender. Uncover and bake an additional 10 minutes. Let stand 5 minutes before serving.

For nutritional information on this recipe, please turn to the appendix on pages 248–251.

from Oxmoor House.

SCAN THIS PHOTO
to see and save
the shopping list.

meal maker

PICK A SIDE DISH

- Waldorf Spinach Salad, page 175

OR

- crusty bread

ADD A DESSERT

- Caramel-Pecan-Pumpkin Bread Puddings, page 233

quick + easy

Bean and Sausage Stew

Makes 4 servings ▪ Prep: 15 minutes ▪ Total: 15 minutes

1 tablespoon olive oil
1 (13-ounce) package chicken sausage links, sliced ¼ inch thick
2 cloves garlic, thinly sliced
1 (19-ounce) can white beans, drained

1 (14.5-ounce) can low-sodium chicken broth
1 (14.5-ounce) can diced tomatoes, undrained
1 bunch kale
¼ teaspoon kosher salt
¼ teaspoon black pepper

1. Heat the oil in a Dutch oven over medium heat. Add the sausage, and cook, without stirring, until browned, about 3 minutes. Turn, add the garlic, and cook for 2 minutes more. Add the beans, broth, and tomatoes and their juices. Increase heat to medium-high, and bring to a simmer.
2. Fold each kale leaf in half lengthwise, and remove the stem by ripping or cutting it. Tear each leaf into large pieces. Add the kale to the pan, and cook, stirring occasionally, until wilted, 2 to 3 minutes. Remove from heat. Season with the salt and pepper, and spoon into individual bowls.

For nutritional information on this recipe, please turn to the appendix on pages 248–251.

from REALSIMPLE

meal maker

PICK A SIDE DISH

- Oven Roasted Sweet Potato Chips with Ranch Dip, page 208

OR

- potato salad

ADD A DESSERT

- Peanut Butter Ice Cream Sandwiches, page 247

quick + easy

Turkey Tenders

Makes 4 servings ▪ Prep: 20 minutes ▪ Total: 30 minutes

1 (1-pound) turkey tenderloin
¼ cup all-purpose flour
⅓ cup egg substitute
¾ cup panko (Japanese breadcrumbs)

2 tablespoons grated Parmesan cheese
¼ teaspoon garlic salt
¼ teaspoon black pepper
1 tablespoon canola oil

1. Preheat oven to 425°.

2. Cut tenderloin in half lengthwise; cut into 20 (2-inch) pieces.

3. Place flour in a shallow dish. Place egg substitute in another. Combine panko, cheese, garlic salt, and pepper in another dish. Dredge turkey in flour; dip in egg substitute, and dredge in breadcrumb mixture. Heat oil in a large nonstick skillet over medium-high heat, swirling to coat. Add turkey pieces to pan; cook 2 minutes on each side. Place turkey pieces on a broiler pan. Bake at 425° for 5 minutes. Turn turkey pieces over, and bake an additional 5 minutes or until golden.

For nutritional information on this recipe, please turn to the appendix on pages 248–251.

from CookingLight

SCAN THIS PHOTO
to see and save
the shopping list.

great for company

Baked Penne with Turkey

Makes 10 servings ▪ Prep: 25 minutes ▪ Total: 1 hour, 10 minutes

12 ounces uncooked penne
(tube-shaped pasta)
1 tablespoon olive oil
2 (8-ounce) packages presliced
mushrooms
2 tablespoons dry sherry
1 cup chopped onion
2 teaspoons minced garlic
1 tablespoon water
5 tablespoons all-purpose flour
3 cups organic vegetable broth
1 cup milk
1 tablespoon fresh thyme leaves

¾ teaspoon salt
½ teaspoon freshly ground black
pepper
¼ cup unsalted butter
4 cups chopped cooked turkey
breast
1 cup frozen petite green peas,
thawed
4 ounces grated fresh Parmesan
cheese (about 1 cup), divided
Cooking spray
Thyme leaves (optional)

1. Preheat oven to 350°.
2. Cook pasta according to package directions, omitting salt and fat.
Drain and return to pan. Cover and keep warm.
3. Heat a large nonstick skillet over medium-high heat. Add oil; swirl
to coat. Add mushrooms; cook 8 minutes or until browned and tender,
stirring occasionally. Stir in sherry, scraping pan to loosen browned bits.
Cook 1 minute or until liquid evaporates. Remove mushrooms from pan.
Add onion and garlic to pan; sauté over medium heat 4 minutes. Add 1
tablespoon water; cook 1 minute or until tender, stirring constantly.
4. Place flour in a large saucepan; gradually add vegetable broth and
next 4 ingredients (through pepper), stirring with a whisk until blended.
Place over medium heat; cook until thickened (about 5 minutes), stirring
constantly. Add butter, stirring until melted. Add sauce, mushrooms,
onion mixture, turkey, peas, and ½ cup cheese to pasta, stirring until
cheese melts. Pour mixture into a 13 x 9–inch glass or ceramic baking
dish coated with cooking spray. Sprinkle with remaining ½ cup cheese.
5. Bake, uncovered, at 350° for 25 minutes. Let stand 5 minutes. Garnish
with thyme, if desired.

For nutritional information on this recipe, please turn to the appendix on pages 248–251.

from Oxmoor House.

meal maker

PICK A SIDE DISH

- Broccoli Rabe with Garlic
and Golden Raisins,
page 161

OR

- steamed broccoli

ADD A DESSERT

- Luscious Lemon Bars,
page 217

QUICK TIP

This dish is a great use of
leftover turkey. If you're
fresh out, substitute
chopped rotisserie chicken
instead.

SCAN THIS PHOTO
to see and save
the shopping list.

great for company

Smoke-Roasted Turkey Breast with Pomegranate-Thyme Glaze

Makes 8 servings ▪ Prep: 30 minutes ▪ Total: 2 hours, 50 minutes

2 cups cherry or apple wood chips
1 (6-pound) whole bone-in turkey breast
1 tablespoon chopped fresh thyme, divided
2 teaspoons kosher salt, divided
1 teaspoon freshly ground black pepper

3 garlic cloves, thinly sliced
1 teaspoon olive oil
1 large shallot, finely chopped
1½ cups pomegranate juice
¼ cup sugar
Cooking spray

1. Soak wood chips in water 1 hour; drain well.
2. Trim excess fat from turkey. Loosen skin from breast by inserting fingers, gently pushing between skin and meat. Combine 2 teaspoons thyme, 1½ teaspoons salt, pepper, and garlic, stirring well. Rub thyme mixture under loosened skin.
3. Heat oil in small saucepan over medium-high heat; swirl to coat. Add remaining 1 teaspoon thyme, remaining ½ teaspoon salt, and shallot; sauté for 2 minutes. Add juice and sugar. Bring to a boil; reduce heat, and simmer 15 minutes or until syrupy and reduced to about ½ cup. Remove from heat.
4. To prepare turkey for indirect grilling, remove grill rack. Preheat the grill to medium-high using both burners. After preheating, turn the left burner off (leave the right burner on). Place 1 cup wood chips on heat element on right side. Place a disposable aluminum foil pan on heat element on left (unheated) side. Pour 2 cups water in pan. Coat grill rack with cooking spray, and place on grill. Place the turkey on grill rack covering left burner. Cover and grill for 1 hour and 20 minutes or until a thermometer registers 165°, turning halfway during cooking time. Add the remaining 1 cup wood chips halfway during cooking time, and brush turkey with half of pomegranate mixture during last 5 minutes of cooking. Place the turkey on a platter. Let stand 30 minutes. Discard skin. Serve with remaining pomegranate mixture.

For nutritional information on this recipe, please turn to the appendix on pages 248–251.

from CookingLight

meal maker

PICK A SIDE DISH

- Bacon-Brown Sugar Brussels Sprouts, page 162

OR

- garlic mashed potatoes

ADD A DESSERT

- Chocolate-Caramel Pecan Pie, page 240

QUICK TIP

You can use fresh or frozen turkey breast as long as it's fully thawed. Turkey breast cooks and thaws faster than a whole bird.

meal maker

PICK A SIDE DISH

- Roasted Squash and Kale Salad, page 173

OR

- French baguette

ADD A DESSERT

- Roasted Banana Bars with Browned Butter–Pecan Frosting, page 219

QUICK TIP

If you can't find walnut oil, substitute a fruity extra-virgin olive oil.

quick + easy

Cassoulet in a Flash

Makes 4 servings ▪ Prep: 30 minutes ▪ Total: 30 minutes

3 ounces duck sausage, casings removed
2 ounces center-cut bacon, cut into ¼-inch pieces
⅓ cup chopped onion
⅓ cup chopped celery
⅓ cup chopped carrot
1 tablespoon chopped fresh thyme
2 garlic cloves, minced
1 (3-ounce) boneless duck breast half
Cooking spray
2 (15.5-ounce) cans no-salt-added white beans, rinsed, drained, and divided

2 tablespoons no-salt-added tomato paste
1¼ cups unsalted chicken stock (such as Swanson)
½ teaspoon freshly ground black pepper
½ cup panko (Japanese breadcrumbs)
1 tablespoon chopped fresh flat-leaf parsley
2 tablespoons walnut oil

1. Preheat the broiler.

2. Heat a large skillet over medium heat. Add sausage and bacon to pan; cook 5 minutes or until lightly browned, stirring occasionally to crumble sausage. Remove mixture from pan using a slotted spoon; place in a bowl. Reserve 1 tablespoon drippings in pan; reserve remaining drippings for another use. Increase heat to medium-high. Add onion and next 4 ingredients (through minced garlic) to drippings in pan; sauté 3 minutes, stirring occasionally. Add onion mixture to sausage mixture.

3. Remove skin from duck breast; discard skin. Cut breast into ½-inch pieces. Return pan to medium-high heat. Lightly coat pan with cooking spray. Add duck breast; sauté for 3 minutes, turning to brown on all sides. Remove from heat.

4. Combine ½ cup beans, tomato paste, and stock in a food processor; process until smooth. Add pureed bean mixture, sausage mixture, remaining beans, and pepper to pan with duck; bring to a boil over medium-high heat. Cook 2 minutes. Spoon 1 cup bean mixture into each of 4 (8-ounce) ramekins lightly coated with cooking spray. Combine panko, parsley, and oil in a small bowl; toss. Divide panko mixture evenly among ramekins. Place ramekins on a baking sheet; broil 2 minutes or until browned.

For nutritional information on this recipe, please turn to the appendix on pages 248–251.

from CookingLight

SCAN THIS PHOTO to see and save the shopping list.

PORK WITH APPLES, BACON,
AND SAUERKRAUT, *page 66*

SCAN THIS PHOTO
to see and save
the shopping list.

meats

Whether you're cooking a budget-friendly meal or something for a special occasion, you're sure to be satisfied when selecting a hearty cut of beef, pork, or lamb for your main dish.

meal maker

PICK A SIDE DISH

- Grilled Zucchini with Sea Salt, page 182

OR

- oven-baked French fries

ADD A DESSERT

- So Good Brownies, page 220

QUICK TIP

Not keen on blue cheese? Substitute another soft cheese like feta or goat cheese instead.

great for company

Caramelized Onion–and– Blue Cheese Mini Burgers

Makes 8 servings ▪ Prep: 20 minutes ▪ Total: 30 minutes

1 medium onion, thinly sliced
Cooking spray
½ teaspoon salt
½ teaspoon freshly ground black pepper
1 pound ground sirloin
2 tablespoons canola mayonnaise
1½ tablespoons crumbled blue cheese
8 slider buns, toasted
1½ cups arugula
8 thin tomato slices

1. Heat a medium nonstick skillet over medium-high heat. Add onion to pan; coat onion with cooking spray. Cook 15 minutes, stirring frequently, until tender and browned. Remove pan from heat. Finely chop ¼ cup onion, and place in a medium bowl, reserving remaining onion in pan.
2. Add salt, pepper, and beef to caramelized onion in bowl; mix well. Divide beef mixture into 8 equal portions, shaping each into a ¼-inch-thick patty.
3. Heat a grill pan over medium-high heat. Place patties on grill pan. Grill 3 minutes on each side, until a thermometer registers 160° or until desired degree of doneness.
4. Place mayonnaise and blue cheese in a food processor; process until smooth. Spread blue cheese mixture evenly on bottom halves of buns. Place 1 patty on bottom half of each bun. Top patties evenly with arugula, tomato slices, and remaining caramelized onion; cover with bun tops.

For nutritional information on this recipe, please turn to the appendix on pages 248–251.

from Cooking Light

quick + easy

Cheesy Meat Loaf Minis

Makes 6 servings ▪ Prep: 10 minutes ▪ Total: 35 minutes

1 ounce fresh breadcrumbs
  (about ½ cup)
Cooking spray
1 cup chopped onion
2 garlic cloves, chopped
½ cup ketchup, divided
¼ cup chopped fresh parsley
2 tablespoons grated Parmesan
  cheese
1 tablespoon prepared
  horseradish

1 tablespoon Dijon mustard
¾ teaspoon dried oregano
¼ teaspoon salt
¼ teaspoon freshly ground black
  pepper
3 ounces white cheddar cheese,
  diced
1½ pounds ground sirloin
1 large egg, lightly beaten

1. Preheat oven to 425°.
2. Heat a skillet over medium-high heat. Add breadcrumbs; cook 3 minutes or until toasted, stirring frequently.
3. While breadcrumbs cook, heat a large skillet over medium-high heat. Coat pan with cooking spray. Add onion and garlic; sauté 3 minutes. Combine onion mixture, breadcrumbs, ¼ cup ketchup, and remaining ingredients. Shape into 6 (4 x 2-inch) loaves on a broiler pan coated with cooking spray; spread 2 teaspoons ketchup over each. Bake at 425° for 25 minutes or until done.

For nutritional information on this recipe, please turn to the appendix on pages 248–251.

from CookingLight

meal maker

PICK A SIDE DISH

• Creamy Grits Casserole,
  page 197

OR

• English peas

ADD A DESSERT

• Real Banana Pudding,
  page 235

meal maker

PICK A SIDE DISH

- Arugula Avocado Salad, page 154

OR

- black beans

ADD A DESSERT

- Last-Minute Tropical Sherbet, page 245

quick + easy

Enchilada Casserole

Makes 4 servings ▪ Prep: 20 minutes ▪ Total: 30 minutes

1 pound ground sirloin
1 cup chopped onion
1 tablespoon butter
1 tablespoon minced garlic
1½ tablespoons all-purpose flour
1 cup fat-free, lower-sodium beef broth
1 tablespoon 25%-less-sodium taco seasoning mix
1 (8-ounce) can no-salt-added tomato sauce
4 (8-inch) whole-wheat flour tortillas
⅓ cup (1½ ounces) shredded Monterey Jack cheese with jalapeño peppers

1. Heat a large nonstick skillet over medium-high heat. Add beef and onion to pan; cook 6 minutes, stirring to crumble.
2. Preheat oven to 400°.
3. Melt butter in a medium saucepan over medium-high heat. Add garlic; sauté 1 minute. Sprinkle with flour; cook 30 seconds, stirring constantly. Add broth, taco seasoning, and tomato sauce to pan. Bring to a boil; cook 2 minutes, stirring occasionally. Add 1½ cups tomato mixture to beef mixture; reserve ½ cup tomato mixture.
4. Place 1 tortilla in a 9-inch pie plate. Top with 1 cup beef mixture. Repeat layers, ending with tortilla. Spread reserved tomato mixture over tortilla. Top with cheese. Bake at 400° for 10 minutes or until cheese melts. Cool slightly. Cut into 4 wedges.

For nutritional information on this recipe, please turn to the appendix on pages 248–251.

from CookingLight

meal maker

PICK A SIDE DISH

- Quinoa with Roasted Garlic, Tomatoes, and Spinach, page 201

OR

- mashed potatoes

ADD A DESSERT

- Chocolate-Caramel Pecan Pie, page 240

healthy choice

Beef Tenderloin Steaks and Balsamic Green Beans

Makes 4 servings ▪ Prep: 10 minutes ▪ Total: 35 minutes

2 teaspoons butter, divided
1 cup vertically sliced yellow onion
1 cup vertically sliced red onion
¼ cup sliced shallots
3 garlic cloves, minced
½ cup fat-free, lower-sodium beef broth
2 cups green beans, trimmed

2 tablespoons balsamic vinegar
¼ teaspoon salt, divided
4 (4-ounce) beef tenderloin steaks
¼ teaspoon freshly ground black pepper
Cooking spray
Fresh flat-leaf parsley (optional)

1. Melt 1 teaspoon butter in a medium saucepan over medium-high heat. Add onions and shallots; sauté 6 minutes. Add garlic; sauté 1 minute. Add broth; cook 4 minutes or until onions are tender and liquid almost evaporates. Add beans and vinegar; cover and cook 4 minutes or until beans are crisp-tender. Remove from heat. Stir in remaining 1 teaspoon butter and ⅛ teaspoon salt; keep warm.

2. Sprinkle steaks with remaining ⅛ teaspoon salt and pepper. Heat a cast-iron skillet over medium-high heat. Coat pan with cooking spray. Add steaks to pan; cook 3 minutes on each side or until desired degree of doneness. Let stand 5 minutes. Garnish with parsley, if desired. Serve with bean mixture.

For nutritional information on this recipe, please turn to the appendix on pages 248–251.

from CookingLight

meal maker

PICK A SIDE DISH

• Roasted Sweet Potatoes and Apples, page 211

OR

• spring rolls

ADD A DESSERT

• Chewy Caramel Apple Cookies, page 214

QUICK TIP

You can make the salad components ahead of time. Just be sure to assemble and add the dressing right before serving.

healthy choice

Thai Beef Salad

Makes 4 servings ▪ Prep: 20 minutes ▪ Total: 25 minutes

Leaves from ½ bunch cilantro
1 package (4 ounces) sprouts, such as radish or pea
½ English cucumber, halved lengthwise and sliced thinly
⅓ cup thinly sliced red onion, rinsed
2 celery stalks, sliced diagonally
2 teaspoons Thai or Vietnamese fish sauce

3 tablespoons Thai sweet chili sauce
Juice of 1 lime
1 tablespoon vegetable oil
½ pound sirloin steak, sliced thinly
2 teaspoons soy sauce

1. Put cilantro, sprouts, cucumber, onion, and celery in a large bowl. In a small bowl, mix together fish sauce, chili sauce, and lime juice to make dressing. Set both aside.

2. Heat oil in a large frying pan over high heat. Add beef and cook, stirring occasionally, until no longer pink, about 4 minutes. Drizzle beef with soy sauce. Add beef to vegetable mixture, pour dressing over salad, and toss gently to combine.

For nutritional information on this recipe, please turn to the appendix on pages 248–251.

from *Sunset*

SCAN THIS PHOTO
to see and save
the shopping list.

meal maker

PICK A SIDE DISH

- Loaded Twice-Baked Potatoes, page 207

OR

- roasted asparagus

ADD A DESSERT

- Flourless Peanut Butter-Chocolate Chip Cookies, page 216

quick + easy

Pan-Grilled Flank Steak with Soy-Mustard Sauce

Makes 4 servings ■ Prep: 10 minutes ■ Total: 20 minutes

1 pound flank steak, trimmed
⅜ teaspoon kosher salt
¼ teaspoon freshly ground black pepper
Cooking spray
1 teaspoon canola oil
1½ teaspoons minced fresh garlic
2 tablespoons lower-sodium soy sauce
1 teaspoon Dijon mustard
¾ teaspoon sugar
1½ tablespoons heavy whipping cream
2 tablespoons chopped fresh cilantro, divided

1. Heat a grill pan over high heat. Sprinkle steak evenly with salt and pepper. Lightly coat the steak with cooking spray. Add steak to pan; grill for 5 minutes on each side or until desired degree of doneness. Let stand 3 minutes.

2. Heat a small skillet over medium-high heat. Add oil to pan; swirl to coat. Add garlic; cook for 30 seconds or until fragrant. Add soy sauce, mustard, and sugar; cook 1 minute or until bubbly. Remove pan from heat. Stir in cream and 1 tablespoon cilantro. Cut steak diagonally across grain into thin slices. Sprinkle with remaining 1 tablespoon cilantro. Serve sauce with steak.

For nutritional information on this recipe, please turn to the appendix on pages 248–251.

from **CookingLight**

Flank Steak Salad with Plums and Blue Cheese

Makes 4 servings ▪ Prep: 10 minutes ▪ Total: 20 minutes

½ teaspoon freshly ground black pepper
¼ teaspoon salt
1½ tablespoons olive oil, divided
4 teaspoons fresh lemon juice, divided
1 (1-pound) flank steak, trimmed
Cooking spray

1 teaspoon honey
⅛ teaspoon salt
8 cups loosely packed baby arugula
3 plums, thinly sliced
¼ cup (1 ounce) crumbled blue cheese

1. Combine pepper, ¼ teaspoon salt, 1½ teaspoons olive oil, and 1 teaspoon lemon juice in a small bowl; rub over both sides of steak.

2. Heat a large skillet over medium-high heat. Coat pan with cooking spray. Add steak to pan; cook 5 minutes on each side or until desired degree of doneness. Remove steak from pan; let rest 5 minutes. Cut steak diagonally across grain into thin slices.

3. Combine remaining 1 tablespoon olive oil, 1 tablespoon lemon juice, honey, and ⅛ teaspoon salt in a large bowl; stir well with a whisk. Add arugula; toss gently to coat. Arrange about 1½ cups arugula mixture on each of 4 plates; top each serving with 3 ounces steak, about ½ cup plums, and 1 tablespoon cheese.

For nutritional information on this recipe, please turn to the appendix on pages 248–251.

from CookingLight

meal maker

PICK A SIDE DISH

• Creamed Silver Queen Corn, page 170

OR

• sliced tomatoes with fresh basil

ADD A DESSERT

• Strawberry-Rhubarb Ice Cream, page 246

meats

meal maker

PICK A SIDE DISH

- Simple Sesame Salad, page 156

OR

- steam-in-the-bag sugar snap peas

ADD A DESSERT

- Honeyed Apples with Ice Cream, page 223

quick + easy

Stir-Fried Beef with Noodles

Makes 4 servings ▪ Prep: 15 minutes ▪ Total: 25 minutes

---

3 cups broccoli florets
8 ounces rice noodles
2 cups low-sodium chicken broth
2 tablespoons green or red curry paste
2 tablespoons fish sauce
2 tablespoons vegetable oil

1 pound flank steak, cut into thin strips
Salt and pepper
1 tablespoon finely chopped fresh ginger
2 cloves garlic, chopped

1. Bring a pot of salted water to a boil. Add broccoli and rice noodles; cook until just tender, about 4 minutes. Drain; rinse under cold water. In a medium bowl, whisk together broth, curry paste, and fish sauce.

2. In a large skillet, warm oil over high heat. Season beef with salt and pepper; add to skillet in a single layer. Cook, stirring, until no longer pink, about 4 minutes. Transfer to a bowl.

3. Add ginger and garlic to skillet; sauté 30 seconds. Add broth mixture, beef, noodles, and broccoli to skillet, and sauté until sauce thickens and ingredients are heated through.

For nutritional information on this recipe, please turn to the appendix on pages 248–251.

from all*you*

Italian Pot Roast

Makes 6 servings ▪ Prep: 10 minutes ▪ Total: 8 hours, 50 minutes

1 (8-ounce) package sliced fresh mushrooms
1 large sweet onion, cut in half and sliced
1 (3- to 4-pound) boneless chuck roast, trimmed
1 teaspoon pepper
2 tablespoons olive oil
1 (1-ounce) envelope dry onion soup mix
1 (14-ounce) can beef broth
1 (8-ounce) can tomato sauce
3 tablespoons tomato paste
1 teaspoon dried Italian seasoning
2 tablespoons cornstarch

1. Place mushrooms and onion in a lightly greased 5- to 6-quart slow cooker.

2. Sprinkle roast with pepper. Cook roast in hot oil in a large skillet over medium-high heat 2 to 3 minutes on each side or until browned.

3. Place roast on top of mushrooms and onion in slow cooker. Sprinkle onion soup mix over roast; pour beef broth and tomato sauce over roast. Cover and cook on LOW 8 to 10 hours or until meat shreds easily with a fork.

4. Transfer roast to a cutting board; cut into large chunks, removing any large pieces of fat. Keep roast warm.

5. Skim fat from juices in slow cooker; stir in tomato paste and Italian seasoning. Stir together cornstarch and 2 tablespoons water in a small bowl until smooth; add to juices in slow cooker, stirring until blended. Increase slow cooker heat to HIGH. Cover and cook 40 minutes or until mixture is thickened. Stir in roast.

from **Southern Living**

meal maker

PICK A SIDE DISH

• Roasted Baby Beet Salad, page 157

OR

• buttered noodles

ADD A DESSERT

• White and Dark Chocolate Pudding Parfaits, page 237

meats

QUICK TIP

Feeling adventurous? Mix up your mushroom selection; try baby portobellos, creminis, or hen-of-the-woods mushrooms.

meal maker

PICK A SIDE DISH

- New-Fashioned Apple Raisin Slaw, page 184

OR

- garlic-cheese bread

ADD A DESSERT

- Caramel-Pecan-Pumpkin Bread Puddings, page 233

QUICK TIP

You can use another dark beer or stout in place of the Guinness.

great for company

Beef and Guinness Stew

Makes 8 servings ▪ Prep: 30 minutes ▪ Total: 3 hours, 20 minutes

3 tablespoons canola oil, divided
¼ cup all-purpose flour
2 pounds boneless chuck roast, trimmed and cut into 1-inch cubes
1 teaspoon salt, divided
5 cups chopped onion (about 3 onions)
1 tablespoon tomato paste
4 cups fat-free, lower-sodium beef broth
1 (11.2-ounce) bottle Guinness Stout
1 tablespoon raisins
1 teaspoon caraway seeds
½ teaspoon black pepper
1½ cups (½-inch-thick) diagonal slices carrot (about 8 ounces)
1½ cups (½-inch-thick) diagonal slices parsnip (about 8 ounces)
1 cup (½-inch) cubed peeled turnip (about 8 ounces)
2 tablespoons finely chopped fresh flat-leaf parsley

1. Heat 1½ tablespoons oil in a Dutch oven over medium-high heat. Place flour in a shallow dish. Sprinkle beef with ½ teaspoon salt; dredge beef in flour. Add half of beef to pan; cook 5 minutes, turning to brown on all sides. Remove beef from pan with a slotted spoon. Repeat procedure with remaining 1½ tablespoons oil and beef.
2. Add onion to pan; cook 5 minutes or until tender, stirring occasionally. Stir in tomato paste; cook 1 minute, stirring frequently. Stir in broth and beer, scraping pan to loosen browned bits. Return meat to pan. Stir in remaining ½ teaspoon salt, raisins, caraway seeds, and pepper; bring to a boil. Cover, reduce heat, and simmer 1 hour, stirring occasionally. Uncover and bring to a boil. Cook 50 minutes, stirring occasionally. Add carrot, parsnip, and turnip. Cover, reduce heat to low, and simmer 30 minutes, stirring occasionally. Uncover and bring to a boil; cook 10 minutes or until vegetables are tender. Sprinkle with parsley.

For nutritional information on this recipe, please turn to the appendix on pages 248–251.

from CookingLight

SCAN THIS PHOTO
to see and save
the shopping list.

meal maker

PICK A SIDE DISH

- Melon Ball Salad with Lime Syrup, page 185

OR

- Caesar salad

ADD A DESSERT

- Peanut Butter Ice Cream Sandwiches, page 247

quick + easy

Pasta Pork Bolognese

Makes 4 servings ▪ Prep: 10 minutes ▪ Total: 20 minutes

9 ounces refrigerated fettuccine
2 teaspoons olive oil
12 ounces lean ground pork
½ cup grated carrot
3 garlic cloves, minced
⅓ cup red wine

1⅔ cups lower-sodium marinara sauce
½ cup chopped fresh basil, divided
½ teaspoon kosher salt
¼ teaspoon black pepper

1. Cook pasta per directions. Drain.
2. Heat olive oil in a large skillet over medium-high heat. Add pork, carrot, and garlic; sauté 4 minutes or until pork is done. Add wine; cook 1 minute. Add marinara, ¼ cup basil, salt, and pepper; bring to a simmer. Pour sauce over pasta. Sprinkle with remaining ¼ cup basil.

For nutritional information on this recipe, please turn to the appendix on pages 248–251.

from CookingLight

healthy choice

Grilled Pork Chops with Two-Melon Salsa

Makes 4 servings ▪ Prep: 20 minutes ▪ Total: 30 minutes

Salsa:
1 cup chopped seedless watermelon
1 cup chopped honeydew melon
3 tablespoons finely chopped sweet onion
1 tablespoon finely chopped jalapeño pepper
1 tablespoon chopped fresh cilantro
1 tablespoon fresh lime juice
⅛ teaspoon salt

Pork chops:
2 teaspoons canola oil
1½ teaspoons chili powder
½ teaspoon garlic powder
½ teaspoon salt
¼ teaspoon freshly ground black pepper
4 (4-ounce) boneless center-cut pork chops, trimmed
Cooking spray

1. To prepare salsa, combine the first 7 ingredients; set aside.
2. To prepare pork chops, heat a grill pan over medium-high heat. Combine oil and next 4 ingredients (through black pepper) in a small bowl. Rub oil mixture over both sides of pork chops. Coat pan with cooking spray. Add pork to pan; cook 4 minutes on each side or until desired degree of doneness. Serve with salsa.

For nutritional information on this recipe, please turn to the appendix on pages 248–251.

from Cooking Light

meal maker

PICK A SIDE DISH

- Grilled Asparagus with Caper Vinaigrette, page 155

OR

- whole-wheat couscous

ADD A DESSERT

- Brown Sugar-Cinnamon Peach Pie, page 238

SCAN THIS PHOTO to see and save the shopping list.

quick + easy

Pork and Tomato Skillet Sauté

Makes 4 servings ▪ Prep: 10 minutes ▪ Total: 15 minutes

4 teaspoons olive oil, divided
4 (6-ounce) bone-in center-cut
   loin pork chops, trimmed
   (about ½ inch thick)
½ teaspoon salt, divided
½ teaspoon freshly ground black
   pepper, divided

½ cup thinly sliced shallots
2 tablespoons balsamic vinegar
2 teaspoons minced garlic
2 cups grape tomatoes
3 tablespoons fresh basil leaves

1. Heat a large nonstick skillet over medium-high heat. Add 1 teaspoon oil; swirl to coat. Sprinkle chops evenly with ¼ teaspoon salt and ¼ teaspoon pepper. Add pork to pan; cook 3 minutes on each side or until desired degree of doneness. Remove pork from pan. Add remaining 1 tablespoon oil, shallots, vinegar, and garlic to pan; sauté 1 minute, scraping pan to loosen browned bits.
2. Combine tomatoes, remaining ¼ teaspoon salt, and remaining ¼ teaspoon pepper in a medium bowl; toss gently to coat. Add tomato mixture to pan; cook 2 minutes or until tomatoes begin to soften. Sprinkle with basil. Serve tomato mixture with pork.

For nutritional information on this recipe, please turn to the appendix on pages 248–251.

from CookingLight

meal maker

PICK A SIDE DISH

- Summer Squash Ribbons
  with Lemon and Parmesan,
  page 177

OR

- orzo tossed with fresh herbs

ADD A DESSERT

- Real Banana Pudding,
  page 235

meal maker

PICK A SIDE DISH

- Creamy Lime Slaw, page 164

OR

- plantain chips

ADD A DESSERT

- Grilled Pound Cake with Lemon Cream and Blueberries, page 232

Cuban Sandwiches

Makes 4 servings ▪ Prep: 10 minutes ▪ Total: 4 hours, 45 minutes

3 tablespoons extra-virgin
   olive oil
½ cup minced onion
½ teaspoon kosher salt
½ teaspoon dried oregano
½ teaspoon freshly ground black
   pepper
6 garlic cloves, minced
¾ cup fresh orange juice (about
   2 oranges)
2 tablespoons fresh lime juice
8 ounces pork tenderloin

Cooking spray
½ cup finely chopped dill pickle
2 tablespoons prepared mustard
2 teaspoons extra-virgin olive oil
4 (3-inch) pieces Cuban bread,
   cut in half horizontally
8 thin slices deli less-sodium ham
   (about 3 ounces)
4 (1-ounce) slices reduced-fat
   Swiss cheese
1 cup baby spinach

1. Heat 3 tablespoons olive oil in a small skillet over medium-high heat. Add onion, salt, oregano, black pepper, and minced garlic; sauté 3 minutes or until onion is tender. Remove from heat; stir in orange juice and lime juice. Reserve 2 tablespoons juice mixture; cover and refrigerate. Combine remaining juice mixture and pork in a large zip-top plastic bag; seal. Marinate pork mixture in refrigerator at least 4 hours or overnight.
2. Prepare grill to medium-high heat.
3. Remove pork from bag; discard marinade. Place pork on grill rack coated with cooking spray; grill 15 minutes or until thermometer registers 145° (slightly pink), turning occasionally. Remove pork from grill. Cover loosely with foil; let stand 10 minutes. Cut pork into 16 thin slices.
4. Combine pickle, reserved 2 tablespoons juice mixture, mustard, and 2 teaspoons oil in a small bowl; stir until well blended.
5. Hollow out top and bottom halves of bread, leaving a ½-inch-thick shell; reserve torn bread for another use. Spread 2 teaspoons pickle mixture over cut side of each half. Arrange 4 pork slices, 2 ham slices, 1 cheese slice, and ¼ cup spinach on each bottom half of bread; cover with top halves.
6. Heat a large nonstick grill pan over medium-high heat. Coat pan with cooking spray. Add sandwiches to pan. Place a cast-iron or heavy skillet on top of sandwiches; gently press to flatten. Leave skillet on; cook 4 minutes on each side or until cheese melts and bread is toasted.

For nutritional information on this recipe, please turn to the appendix on pages 248–251.

from CookingLight

SCAN THIS PHOTO to see and save the shopping list.

meal maker

PICK A SIDE DISH

- Three-Bean Salad, page 188

OR

- grilled summer vegetables

ADD A DESSERT

- Luscious Lemon Bars, page 217

healthy choice

Pork Tenderloin Salad and Grilled Nectarines

Makes 4 servings ▪ Prep: 10 minutes ▪ Total: 45 minutes

5 tablespoons olive oil
3 tablespoons balsamic vinegar
2 teaspoons minced fresh tarragon
2 garlic cloves, minced
2 tablespoons maple syrup, divided
1 (1-pound) pork tenderloin, trimmed

½ teaspoon kosher salt
¼ teaspoon freshly ground black pepper
Cooking spray
2 large nectarines, halved and pitted
6 cups gourmet salad greens
½ cup thinly sliced red onion

1. Preheat grill to medium-high heat.
2. Combine first 4 ingredients in a small bowl. Divide mixture in half. Combine half of balsamic mixture with 1 tablespoon maple syrup. Reserve 2 tablespoons maple syrup mixture. Brush remaining maple syrup mixture evenly over pork; sprinkle pork with salt and pepper. Place pork on a grill rack coated with cooking spray; grill 16 minutes or until desired degree of doneness, turning occasionally and brushing with reserved maple syrup mixture. Remove pork from grill, and let stand 10 minutes before slicing.
3. Coat cut sides of nectarines with cooking spray; brush with remaining 1 tablespoon maple syrup. Place, cut sides down, on grill rack; grill 5 minutes or until well marked and tender. Remove from grill; slice into ½-inch wedges.
4. Combine remaining half of balsamic mixture, greens, and onion in a large bowl, tossing to coat. Divide mixture among 4 plates; top with pork and nectarines.

For nutritional information on this recipe, please turn to the appendix on pages 248–251.

from CookingLight

healthy choice

Spiced Pork Tenderloin with Sautéed Apples

Makes 4 servings ▪ Prep: 10 minutes ▪ Total: 20 minutes

⅜ teaspoon salt
¼ teaspoon ground coriander
¼ teaspoon freshly ground black
 pepper
⅛ teaspoon ground cinnamon
⅛ teaspoon ground nutmeg
1 pound pork tenderloin,
 trimmed and cut crosswise
 into 12 pieces

Cooking spray
2 tablespoons butter
2 cups thinly sliced unpeeled
 Braeburn or Gala apple
⅓ cup thinly sliced shallots
⅛ teaspoon salt
¼ cup apple cider
1 teaspoon fresh thyme leaves

1. Heat a large cast-iron skillet over medium-high heat. Combine first 5 ingredients; sprinkle spice mixture evenly over pork. Coat pan with cooking spray. Add pork to pan; cook 3 minutes on each side or until desired degree of doneness. Remove pork from pan; keep warm.
2. Melt butter in pan; swirl to coat. Add apple slices, shallots, and ⅛ teaspoon salt; sauté 4 minutes or until apple starts to brown. Add apple cider to pan, and cook for 2 minutes or until apple is crisp-tender. Stir in thyme leaves. Serve apple mixture with the pork.

For nutritional information on this recipe, please turn to the appendix on pages 248–251.

from CookingLight

meal maker

PICK A SIDE DISH

- Roasted Squash and Kale Salad, page 173

OR

- roasted new potato wedges

ADD A DESSERT

- Red Velvet Cupcakes, page 230

meats

meal maker

PICK A SIDE DISH

- Sausage and Sourdough Bread Stuffing, page 194

OR

- garlic mashed potatoes

ADD A DESSERT

- Caramel-Pecan-Pumpkin Bread Puddings, page 233

QUICK TIP

Look for pancetta, which is smoked Italian bacon cured with salt and spices, in the deli section of your supermarket. If you can't find it, you can substitute thin-cut smoked bacon.

great for company

Pork with Apples, Bacon, and Sauerkraut

Makes 6 to 8 servings ▪ Prep: 50 minutes ▪ Total: 4 hours

1 (3-pound) boneless pork loin
½ teaspoon kosher salt
½ teaspoon freshly ground pepper
6 ounces thinly sliced pancetta or bacon
Kitchen string
2 tablespoons olive oil
2 small onions, quartered (root end intact)
1 (12-ounce) package frozen pearl onions (about 2 cups)
2 garlic cloves, thinly sliced
3 fresh thyme sprigs

2 bay leaves
1 (12-ounce) bottle stout or porter beer
2 tablespoons Dijon mustard
3 firm apples (such as Gala), divided
2 cups jarred sauerkraut, rinsed
2 cups finely shredded green cabbage
1 tablespoon chopped fresh flat-leaf parsley
1 teaspoon fresh lemon juice
½ cup apricot preserves
¼ cup chicken broth

1. Trim fat and silver skin from pork. Sprinkle pork with kosher salt and pepper. Wrap top and sides of pork with pancetta. Tie with kitchen string, securing at 1-inch intervals.

2. Cook pork in hot oil in a large skillet over medium heat, turning occasionally, 15 minutes or until deep golden brown. Remove from skillet, reserving drippings in skillet.

3. Place quartered onion and next 4 ingredients in a 6-quart slow cooker; top with pork.

4. Add beer to reserved drippings in skillet, and cook over medium heat 8 minutes or until liquid is reduced by half, stirring to loosen brown bits from bottom of skillet. Stir in mustard, and pour over pork. Cover and cook on HIGH 2 hours.

5. Peel 2 apples, and cut into large wedges. Add apple wedges, sauerkraut, and cabbage to slow cooker; cover and cook 1 to 2 more hours or until a meat thermometer inserted into thickest portion of pork registers 145° and apples are tender. Remove and discard bay leaves.

6. Cut remaining unpeeled apple into thin strips, and toss with parsley and lemon juice. Season with salt and pepper to taste.

7. Combine preserves and broth in a small saucepan, and cook over medium heat, stirring often, 4 to 5 minutes or until melted and smooth.

8. Brush pork with apricot mixture. Cut pork into slices, and serve with onion mixture, apple-parsley mixture, and additional Dijon mustard, if desired.

from **Southern Living**

SCAN THIS PHOTO
to see and save
the shopping list.

meats

SCAN THIS PHOTO
to see and save
the shopping list.

great for company

Pork Roast with Carolina Gravy

Makes 8 servings ▪ Prep: 25 minutes ▪ Total: 3 hours, 45 minutes

4 medium leeks
1 (5- to 6-pound) bone-in pork
    shoulder roast (Boston butt)
Kitchen string
2 teaspoons salt
2 teaspoons pepper
3 thick bacon slices, chopped
1 tablespoon vegetable oil
10 garlic cloves, halved

3 medium onions, halved and
    sliced
2½ cups low-sodium chicken
    broth
½ cup dry white wine
10 fresh thyme sprigs
4 bay leaves
1 tablespoon butter
Fresh thyme sprigs

1. Preheat oven to 350°. Remove and discard root ends and dark green tops of leeks. Thinly slice leeks; rinse well, and drain.

2. Tie pork roast with kitchen string, securing at 2-inch intervals. Season with salt and pepper.

3. Cook bacon in hot oil in an ovenproof Dutch oven or large, deep cast-iron skillet over medium-high heat 3 minutes. Add leeks, garlic, and onion, and cook, stirring frequently, 15 to 17 minutes or until mixture is golden brown; transfer to a bowl.

4. Add pork roast, fat side down, to Dutch oven, and cook 2 minutes on all sides or until browned. Remove pork.

5. Return leek mixture to Dutch oven; top with pork. Add broth and next 3 ingredients. Reduce heat to medium, and bring to a light boil. Remove from heat, and cover with heavy-duty aluminum foil.

6. Bake at 350° for 3 to 3½ hours or until a meat thermometer inserted into thickest portion registers 180° to 185°. Remove pork from Dutch oven, cover with foil, and let stand 20 minutes before slicing.

7. Meanwhile, pour pan juices through a wire mesh strainer into a saucepan to equal 4 cups, discarding solids (add equal parts broth and white wine to pan juices to equal 4 cups, if necessary). Let stand 5 minutes; skim fat from surface of pan juices.

8. Bring to a boil over medium-high heat, and cook 20 to 25 minutes or until liquid is reduced to 1 cup and slightly thickened. Remove from heat, and stir in butter until melted. Serve with pork and thyme sprigs.

from **Southern Living**

meal maker

PICK A SIDE DISH

- Marinated Greek-Style Pasta, page 198

OR

- coleslaw

ADD A DESSERT

- Mini Berry Cobblers, page 224

QUICK TIP

If you don't own an instant-read thermometer, it's worth purchasing one for this recipe. Cooking this budget-friendly roast to between 180° and 185° ensures incredibly tender slices.

meal maker

PICK A SIDE DISH

- Garlic-Roasted Kale, page 174

OR

- sautéed summer squash

ADD A DESSERT

- White and Dark Chocolate Pudding Parfaits, page 237

quick + easy

Country Ham Carbonara

Makes 4 servings ▪ Prep: 30 minutes ▪ Total: 30 minutes

1 (9-ounce) package refrigerated fettuccine
¾ cup chopped country ham
2 tablespoons olive oil
2 shallots, thinly sliced
2 garlic cloves, pressed
2 pasteurized egg yolks
½ cup (2 ounces) freshly shredded Parmesan cheese
3 tablespoons chopped fresh chives
3 tablespoons chopped fresh parsley
½ teaspoon freshly cracked pepper

1. Cook pasta according to package directions; drain, reserving 1½ cups hot pasta water.

2. Cook ham in hot oil in a large skillet over medium-high heat 4 to 5 minutes or until crisp. Remove ham, reserving drippings in skillet. Drain on paper towels.

3. Sauté shallots in hot drippings 3 to 4 minutes or until tender. Stir in garlic; sauté 1 minute. Add reserved pasta water to shallots and garlic; bring to boil. Stir in hot cooked pasta, and remove from heat. Stir in egg yolks, 1 at a time.

4. Reduce heat to medium, and cook, stirring constantly, 2 to 3 minutes or until creamy. Remove from heat; add cooked ham, Parmesan cheese, and remaining ingredients. Sprinkle with additional Parmesan cheese, if desired. Serve immediately.

from **Southern Living**

SCAN THIS PHOTO
to see and save
the shopping list.

meal maker

PICK A SIDE DISH

- Broccoli Slaw with Candied Pecans, page 158

OR

- potato salad

ADD A DESSERT

- Key Lime Ice Cream Pie, page 243

QUICK TIP

The ribs and glaze will drip as they cook, so prevent a sticky mess in your grill by putting a sturdy drip pan under the cooking grate.

great for company

Grilled Baby Back Ribs with Sticky Brown Sugar Glaze

Makes 8 servings ▪ Prep: 30 minutes ▪ Total: 3 hours

---

5 pounds pork baby back ribs, cut into half-racks if needed to fit on grill
4 teaspoons kosher salt

1½ teaspoons freshly ground black pepper
1 teaspoon cayenne pepper
Sticky Brown Sugar Glaze

1. Remove the membrane from underside of ribs: Slide a screwdriver tip along each bone and under one end of membrane to loosen, then grab membrane with a paper towel and pull off.

2. In a small bowl, mix salt, black pepper, and cayenne pepper. Put ribs on a baking sheet and sprinkle both sides with salt mixture. Snugly wrap each rack in heavy-duty foil. Let stand 30 minutes at room temperature.

3. Meanwhile, prepare a charcoal or gas grill for indirect medium-low heat (300° to 350°; you should be able to hold your hand 5 inches above cooking grate only 6 to 7 seconds). If using charcoal, light 60 briquets in a chimney on firegrate. When coals are covered with ash, about 20 minutes, bank evenly on opposite sides of firegrate and let burn to medium-low. Set a sturdy drip pan on grate between mounds. The area over the drip pan is the indirect heat area. Add 3 or 4 more unlit briquets to each mound when ribs go on and every 30 minutes while cooking. If using gas, turn all burners to high, close lid, and heat 10 minutes. Then turn center burner(s) off and reduce heat of other burner(s) to medium-low. Place a sturdy drip pan under the turned-off burner(s). The area above the drip pan is the indirect heat area.

4. Place rib packets, bone side down, on cooking grate over indirect heat, overlapping slightly if necessary. Cover grill and cook ribs until fairly tender when pierced through foil, 50 to 70 minutes.

5. Transfer rib packets to a rimmed pan. Carefully remove ribs from foil. Set ribs, bone side up, on grill over indirect heat.

6. Spoon about ¼ cup glaze into a small bowl and set aside. Using a silicone brush, baste ribs with remaining glaze. Cover grill and cook ribs 10 minutes. Brush melted glaze from center of each rack up along sides of meat, turn ribs over, and baste with more glaze. Repeat brushing and turning every 10 minutes until ribs are browned and tender and meat has shrunk back from ends of the bones, 30 to 40 minutes total.

7. Remove ribs from grill. Cover loosely with foil and let stand about 10 minutes. Stir reserved ¼ cup glaze and brush over ribs. Cut between bones to serve.

Sticky Brown Sugar Glaze

Makes about 1 cup ▪ Prep: 5 minutes ▪ Total: 5 minutes

1½ cups packed light brown
   sugar
3 tablespoons cider vinegar
3 tablespoons beer or water

1½ teaspoons red chile flakes
   (½ teaspoon for a mild
   version)
1 teaspoon dry mustard

1. In a medium bowl, whisk together all ingredients.

For nutritional information on this recipe, please turn to the appendix on pages 248–251.

from **Sunset**

SCAN THIS PHOTO
to see and save
the shopping list.

Indian-Spiced Lentils and Lamb

Makes 4 servings ▪ Prep: 30 minutes ▪ Total: 1 hour, 10 minutes

2 teaspoons olive oil
6 ounces lean ground lamb
1 teaspoon red curry powder
1 teaspoon ground cumin
½ teaspoon kosher salt
¼ teaspoon ground red pepper
1½ cups chopped onion
¾ cup chopped carrot
1 jalapeño pepper, chopped
5 garlic cloves, minced
1 tablespoon tomato paste

¾ cup brown lentils
2 cups fat-free, lower-sodium chicken broth
1 cup water
¾ cup light coconut milk
1 (15-ounce) can whole peeled tomatoes, drained and coarsely chopped
¼ cup 2% reduced-fat Greek yogurt
¼ cup cilantro leaves

1. Heat a saucepan over medium-high heat. Add oil to pan; swirl. Add lamb and next 4 ingredients (through red pepper); sauté 4 minutes, stirring to crumble. Add onion, carrot, and jalapeño; sauté 4 minutes or until lamb is browned. Add garlic; sauté 1 minute, stirring constantly. Stir in tomato paste; sauté 30 seconds.
2. Add lentils; sauté 30 seconds. Stir in broth and next 3 ingredients (through tomatoes); bring to a boil. Reduce heat, and simmer for 40 minutes or until lentils are tender. Ladle about 1 cup lentil mixture into each of 4 bowls; top each serving with 1 tablespoon yogurt and 1 tablespoon cilantro.

For nutritional information on this recipe, please turn to the appendix on pages 248–251.

from Cooking Light

meal maker

PICK A SIDE DISH

- Curried Cauliflower with Capers, page 167

OR

- steamed bok choy

ADD A DESSERT

- Bittersweet Fudge with Sea Salt, page 222

QUICK TIP

This recipe makes 4 servings but can easily be doubled and made ahead to feed a crowd. Store in an airtight container in the refrigerator for up to 3 days. Top with yogurt and cilantro just before serving.

quick + easy

Greek Lamb Chops and Mint Yogurt Sauce

Makes 4 servings ▪ Prep: 10 minutes ▪ Total: 20 minutes

2 tablespoons fresh lemon juice
2 teaspoons chopped fresh
  oregano
2 garlic cloves, minced
8 (4-ounce) lamb loin chops,
  trimmed
¼ teaspoon kosher salt
¼ teaspoon freshly ground black
  pepper

2 teaspoons canola oil
½ cup plain fat-free yogurt
1 tablespoon chopped fresh mint
½ teaspoon fresh lemon juice
⅛ teaspoon kosher salt
1 garlic clove, minced

1. Combine the first 3 ingredients in a small bowl. Sprinkle lamb with ¼ teaspoon salt and pepper; rub with oregano mixture. Heat a large skillet over high heat. Add oil to pan, swirling to coat. Add lamb, and cook for 3 minutes on each side or until desired degree of doneness. Let stand for 5 minutes.
2. Combine yogurt and remaining ingredients in a small bowl. Serve sauce with lamb.

For nutritional information on this recipe, please turn to the appendix on pages 248–251.

from CookingLight

meal maker

PICK A SIDE DISH

• Bulgur Wheat Salad with Tomato and Eggplant, page 193

OR

• sautéed Broccolini

ADD A DESSERT

• Free-form Strawberry Cheesecake, page 229

meats

QUICK TIP

If you have trouble finding the right size lamb loin chops, ask the butcher to cut them to the size you need. For a thicker sauce, use Greek-style yogurt.

meal maker

PICK A SIDE DISH

- Steamed Carrots with Garlic-Ginger Butter, page 163

OR

- steam-in-the-bag green beans

ADD A DESSERT

- Cherry-Almond Crisp, page 227

quick + easy

Roast Leg of Lamb with Chile-Garlic Sauce

Makes 4 servings ▪ Prep: 10 minutes ▪ Total: 45 minutes

Lamb:
1 (1-pound) boneless leg of lamb, trimmed
¾ teaspoon salt
½ teaspoon freshly ground black pepper
Cooking spray

Sauce:
1 tablespoon sambal oelek (ground fresh chile paste)
½ teaspoon ground cumin
¼ teaspoon ground coriander
⅛ teaspoon salt
3 garlic cloves, minced
2 tablespoons olive oil

1. Preheat oven to 425°.

2. To prepare lamb, sprinkle lamb evenly with ¾ teaspoon salt and pepper. Place lamb on a broiler pan coated with cooking spray. Bake at 425° for 21 minutes or until a thermometer inserted in thickest part of roast registers 120°. Place lamb on a cutting board; let stand at room temperature 10 minutes before slicing.

3. To prepare sauce, combine sambal oelek and next 4 ingredients (through garlic) with a mortar and pestle; grind into a fine paste. Slowly drizzle oil into sambal mixture, stirring until thoroughly combined. Serve sauce with lamb.

For nutritional information on this recipe, please turn to the appendix on pages 248–251.

from CookingLight

QUICK TIP

Sambal oelek is a spicy red chile paste popular in Indonesia, Malaysia, and southern India. Look for it in the spice aisle and in Asian markets. Use it in any dish that needs a little kick. If you can't find it, you can use a sriracha or another chile paste.

SCAN THIS PHOTO to see and save the shopping list.

ARCTIC CHAR AND VEGETABLES
IN PARCHMENT HEARTS, page 86

SCAN THIS PHOTO
to see and save
the shopping list.

fish & shellfish

These fish and shellfish recipes are easy to prepare and pair well with an array of fresh veggies, making them a guaranteed family favorite.

meal maker

PICK A SIDE DISH

- Grilled Corn Poblano Salad with Chipotle Vinaigrette, page 169

OR

- black beans with cilantro

ADD A DESSERT

- Grilled Pound Cake with Lemon Cream and Blueberries, page 232

quick + easy

Grilled Fish Tacos with Tomato-Green Onion Relish

Makes 4 servings ▪ Prep: 10 minutes ▪ Total: 30 minutes

1 tablespoon fresh lime juice
2 teaspoons canola oil
2 garlic cloves, minced
2 teaspoons chili powder
¾ teaspoon ground cumin
¼ teaspoon salt
¼ teaspoon freshly ground black pepper
⅛ teaspoon ground cayenne pepper
1 pound firm white fish fillets
8 (6-inch) fat-free whole-wheat tortillas
Tomato-Green Onion Relish
Lime wedges

1. Combine first 8 ingredients in a bowl. Add fish; toss to coat. Cover and refrigerate 15 minutes.
2. Preheat grill to medium-high heat (350° to 400°). Wrap tortillas in foil. Place fish and tortillas on a grill rack coated with cooking spray. Grill, covered with grill lid, 3 minutes on each side or until fish flakes easily with a fork.
3. Divide fish among tortillas; top with relish. Serve with lime wedges.

Tomato-Green Onion Relish

Makes about 3 cups ▪ Prep: 10 minutes ▪ Total: 10 minutes

2 cups chopped tomatoes
¼ cup sliced green onions
1 jalapeño chile, seeded and minced
¼ cup chopped fresh cilantro
1 tablespoon fresh lime juice
¼ teaspoon salt

1. Combine ingredients in a medium bowl; stir well.

from COASTAL LIVING

SCAN THIS PHOTO to see and save the shopping list.

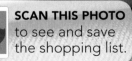

SCAN THIS PHOTO
to see and save
the shopping list.

quick + easy

Open-Faced Blackened Catfish Sandwiches

Makes 4 servings ▪ Prep: 10 minutes ▪ Total: 20 minutes

1¾ teaspoons paprika
1 teaspoon dried oregano
¾ teaspoon ground red pepper
¼ teaspoon salt
¼ teaspoon freshly ground black
   pepper
4 (6-ounce) catfish fillets
2 teaspoons olive oil

⅓ cup plain fat-free Greek yogurt
3 tablespoons fresh lime juice
1 tablespoon honey
2 cups packaged cabbage-carrot
   coleslaw
1 cup chopped fresh cilantro
4 (1-ounce) slices sourdough
   bread, toasted

1. Combine first 5 ingredients in a small bowl. Sprinkle both sides of fish with paprika mixture. Heat a large cast-iron skillet over high heat. Add oil to pan; swirl to coat. Add fish; cook 4 minutes on each side or until desired degree of doneness.

2. Combine yogurt, juice, and honey in a medium bowl. Add cabbage and cilantro; toss well to coat. Top each bread slice with about ½ cup slaw and 1 fillet. Top each fillet with remaining slaw.

For nutritional information on this recipe, please turn to the appendix on pages 248–251.

from CookingLight

meal maker

PICK A SIDE DISH

- Oven Roasted Sweet Potato Chips with Ranch Dip, page 208

OR

- fruit salad

ADD A DESSERT

- Real Banana Pudding, page 235

fish & shellfish

meal maker

PICK A SIDE DISH

- Brown Rice Pilaf with Almonds and Parsley, page 203

OR

- mixed green salad

ADD A DESSERT

- White and Dark Chocolate Pudding Parfaits, page 237

QUICK TIP

If arctic char is not available from your fishmonger, you can substitute frozen wild Alaskan salmon.

healthy choice

Arctic Char and Vegetables in Parchment Hearts

Makes 2 servings ▪ Prep: 15 minutes ▪ Total: 30 minutes

1½ tablespoons unsalted butter, softened
1 teaspoon grated lemon rind
1 tablespoon fresh lemon juice
1 teaspoon chopped fresh dill
2 (6-ounce) arctic char fillets (about 1 inch thick)

¼ teaspoon kosher salt
⅛ teaspoon black pepper
¼ cup julienne-cut leeks
¼ cup julienne-cut red bell pepper
¼ cup julienne-cut carrot
¼ cup julienne-cut snow peas

1. Preheat oven to 450°.
2. Combine first 4 ingredients in a small bowl; stir until blended.
3. Cut 2 (15 x 24-inch) pieces of parchment paper. Fold in half crosswise. Draw a large heart half on each piece, with the fold of the paper along the center of the heart. Cut out the heart, and open. Sprinkle both sides of fillets with salt and pepper. Place one fillet near fold of each parchment heart. Top each fillet with half the vegetables and half the butter mixture. Start at the top of the heart and fold edges of parchment, sealing edges with narrow folds. Twist the end tip to secure tightly. Place packets on a baking sheet. Bake at 450° for 15 minutes. Place on plates; cut open. Serve immediately.

For nutritional information on this recipe, please turn to the appendix on pages 248–251.

from CookingLight

SCAN THIS PHOTO
to see and save
the shopping list.

PICK A SIDE DISH

- Home Fries, page 204

OR

- corn on the cob

ADD A DESSERT

- Flourless Peanut Butter-Chocolate Chip Cookies, page 216

quick + easy

Chip-Crusted Fish Fillets

Makes 4 servings ▪ Prep: 5 minutes ▪ Total: 15 minutes

---

4 (6-ounce) cod fillets (or other firm white fish)
2 teaspoons canola mayonnaise
⅛ teaspoon salt

1 (2-ounce) package salt and vinegar kettle-style potato chips, crushed
½ cup light ranch dressing

1. Preheat oven to 400°.
2. Arrange fillets on a parchment-lined baking sheet. Brush ½ teaspoon mayonnaise over top of each fillet; sprinkle evenly with salt. Gently press about 2 tablespoons crushed chips evenly on top of each fillet. Bake at 400° for 10 minutes or until fish flakes easily when tested with a fork. Serve with ranch dressing.

For nutritional information on this recipe, please turn to the appendix on pages 248–251.

from CookingLight

SCAN THIS PHOTO to see and save the shopping list.

SCAN THIS PHOTO to see and save the shopping list.

quick + easy

Pan-Seared Grouper with Romaine Slaw

Makes 4 servings ▪ Prep: 15 minutes ▪ Total: 30 minutes

2 fresh poblano chiles (or green bell peppers)
1 small jalapeño, seeded and coarsely chopped
2 cups fresh cilantro leaves
Juice from 3 limes (about ¼ cup)
1 tablespoon honey
1¼ teaspoons kosher salt
¼ cup plus 2 tablespoons extra-virgin olive oil
4 (6-ounce) skinless grouper fillets
½ teaspoon freshly ground black pepper
6 ounces tortilla chips
2 heads romaine lettuce, thinly sliced crosswise

1. Heat broiler. Cut each poblano in half lengthwise and remove the stems, seeds, and veins. Place cut-side down on a foil-lined baking sheet. Broil until the skins blacken, about 5 minutes. Transfer to a bowl and cover with plastic wrap for a few minutes. Remove and discard the skins. Slice the poblanos into long, thin strips and place in a medium bowl.
2. In a blender, pulse the jalapeño, cilantro, lime juice, honey, and ¾ teaspoon of the salt to combine. With the motor running, slowly add ¼ cup of the oil and mix until a smooth vinaigrette forms.
3. Heat the remaining oil in a large skillet over medium heat. Season the fish with the remaining salt and the pepper. Cook until the fish is opaque throughout, about 5 minutes per side. Add the poblanos and chips to the lettuce, drizzle with the vinaigrette, and toss. Serve alongside the fish.

For nutritional information on this recipe, please turn to the appendix on pages 248–251.

from **REALSIMPLE**

meal maker

PICK A SIDE DISH

• Buttery Lemon Broccolini, page 160

OR

• polenta

ADD A DESSERT

• Mini Berry Cobblers, page 224

QUICK TIP

You can use any firm, white-fleshed fish in place of the grouper. Try cod, red snapper, halibut, tilapia, or sea bass.

meal maker

PICK A SIDE DISH

- Quinoa with Roasted Garlic, Tomatoes, and Spinach, page 201

OR

- roasted green beans

ADD A DESSERT

- Last-Minute Tropical Sherbet, page 245

quick + easy

Halibut with Smoky Orange Vinaigrette

Makes 4 servings ▪ Prep: 10 minutes ▪ Total: 20 minutes

2 tablespoons orange marmalade
2 tablespoons olive oil
1 tablespoon white wine vinegar
1 tablespoon orange juice
1 tablespoon minced fresh flat-leaf parsley
½ teaspoon salt, divided

½ teaspoon smoked paprika, divided
4 (6-ounce) firm fish fillets such as halibut, snapper, or salmon
2 teaspoons olive oil
¼ teaspoon pepper

1. Combine first 5 ingredients, ⅛ teaspoon salt, and ¼ teaspoon paprika in a medium bowl. Set aside.

2. Brush fish on both sides with olive oil, and sprinkle with pepper and remaining salt and paprika.

3. Heat a nonstick or cast-iron skillet over medium-high heat; add fish, and cook 4 minutes on each side or until fish flakes easily with a fork.

4. Drizzle reserved vinaigrette over cooked fish.

from COASTAL LIVING

meal maker

PICK A SIDE DISH

- Broccoli Slaw with Candied Pecans, page 158

OR

- veggie chips

ADD A DESSERT

- Chewy Caramel Apple Cookies, page 214

quick + easy

Smoked Salmon Sandwich on Pumpernickel

Makes 2 servings ▪ Prep: 15 minutes ▪ Total: 15 minutes

4 slices pumpernickel bread
½ cup crème fraîche or low-fat cream cheese
½ small English cucumber, thinly sliced
¼ small red onion, thinly sliced
1 (4-ounce) package smoked sockeye salmon
2 teaspoons capers
Freshly ground pepper

1. Spread bread slices on 1 side with crème fraîche. Top 2 slices with cucumber, onion, and salmon. Sprinkle with capers and freshly ground pepper. Top with remaining 2 bread slices.

from COASTAL LIVING

QUICK TIP

English cucumbers are time-savers. Because they are seedless and they have thin skins, you won't have to core or peel them before slicing.

quick + easy

Cedar Plank-Grilled Salmon with Mango Kiwi Salsa

Makes 4 servings ▪ Prep: 25 minutes ▪ Total: 40 minutes

1 large cedar plank
1 cup finely diced peeled ripe
  mango
½ cup diced peeled kiwifruit
2 tablespoons chopped fresh
  cilantro
1 teaspoon extra-virgin olive oil
1 teaspoon fresh lime juice

1 serrano chile, finely chopped
½ teaspoon kosher salt, divided
½ teaspoon freshly ground black
  pepper, divided
4 (6-ounce) sustainable skinless
  salmon fillets (such as wild
  Alaskan)

1. Soak plank in water for 25 minutes.
2. Preheat grill to medium-high heat.
3. Combine mango and next 5 ingredients (through chile). Add ¼ teaspoon salt and ¼ teaspoon pepper; set aside.
4. Sprinkle salmon with remaining ¼ teaspoon salt and remaining ¼ teaspoon pepper. Place plank on grill rack; grill 3 minutes or until lightly charred. Turn plank over; place fish on charred side. Cover; grill 8 minutes or until desired degree of doneness. Place each fillet on a plate; top each with ⅓ cup mango salsa.

For nutritional information on this recipe, please turn to the appendix on pages 248–251.

from CookingLight

QUICK TIP

Prepare the mango kiwi salsa before the salmon so the flavors have time to blend.

SCAN THIS PHOTO to see and save the shopping list.

meal maker

PICK A SIDE DISH

- Mozzarella, Tomato, and Basil Salad, page 179

OR

- roasted new potatoes

ADD A DESSERT

- Bittersweet Fudge with Sea Salt, page 222

quick + easy

Tilapia Piccata

Makes 4 servings ▪ Prep: 10 minutes ▪ Total: 20 minutes

---

4 tilapia fillets (about 6 ounces each)
Salt
¼ cup all-purpose flour
2 tablespoons olive oil
3 tablespoons unsalted butter

½ cup white wine
¼ cup lemon juice
1 tablespoon capers
2 tablespoons finely chopped fresh parsley

1. Sprinkle fish lightly with salt and dredge in flour on both sides to coat. Warm 1 tablespoon each oil and butter in a large skillet over medium-high heat until butter melts. Sauté 2 fillets, turning once, until browned on both sides and cooked through, 3 to 4 minutes total. Transfer to a plate; cover with foil to keep warm. Repeat with another tablespoon oil and butter and remaining fish.

2. Pour wine and lemon juice into skillet and bring to a boil. Remove from heat and stir in capers, parsley, and remaining 1 tablespoon butter; keep stirring until butter melts. Place each fillet on a plate, pour sauce over fish, and serve immediately.

For nutritional information on this recipe, please turn to the appendix on pages 248–251.

from **all you**

meal maker

PICK A SIDE DISH

- Broccoli Rabe with Garlic and Golden Raisins, page 161

OR

- napa cabbage slaw

ADD A DESSERT

- Honeyed Apples with Ice Cream, page 223

quick + easy

Sesame Tuna with Edamame and Soba

Makes 4 servings ▪ Prep: 10 minutes ▪ Total: 30 minutes

4 ounces soba (Japanese buckwheat noodles)
1 cup frozen shelled edamame (green soybeans)
2 tablespoons lower-sodium soy sauce
1½ tablespoons fresh lime juice
1½ tablespoons sweet chili sauce
1 tablespoon dark sesame oil
¼ cup chopped fresh cilantro
1 tablespoon white sesame seeds
1 tablespoon black sesame seeds
4 (6-ounce) U.S. yellowfin or albacore tuna steaks
Cooking spray
½ teaspoon kosher salt
2 teaspoons canola oil

1. Cook soba noodles according to package directions, omitting salt and fat; add edamame for last 3 minutes. Rinse with warm water; drain well.
2. Combine soy sauce, lime juice, chili sauce, and sesame oil in a medium bowl. Add soba mixture and cilantro; keep warm.
3. Combine white and black sesame seeds in a shallow dish. Coat tuna with cooking spray, and sprinkle evenly with salt. Coat both sides of each steak with sesame seeds, pressing gently to adhere. Heat a large nonstick skillet over medium-high heat. Add oil to pan; swirl to coat. Add steaks to pan; cook for 3 minutes on each side or until desired degree of doneness. Slice tuna thinly against grain. Serve with noodles.

For nutritional information on this recipe, please turn to the appendix on pages 248–251.

from Cooking Light

SCAN THIS PHOTO
to see and save
the shopping list.

healthy choice

Tuna Niçoise Salad with Roasted Green Beans and Potatoes

Makes 4 servings ▪ Prep: 10 minutes ▪ Total: 35 minutes

8 ounces small potatoes, such as Red Bliss or fingerling (about 9), halved
8 ounces green beans, trimmed
2 tablespoons plus 2 teaspoons olive oil, divided
¼ teaspoon salt, divided
¼ teaspoon pepper, divided
2 tablespoons fresh lemon juice
1 tablespoon capers, rinsed
1 tablespoon chopped fresh parsley

1 large head oak leaf lettuce (about 12 loosely packed cups)
1 (6-ounce) can tuna in olive oil, drained
¼ cup olives, such as oil-cured or kalamata, pitted and halved
1 cup halved grape tomatoes (about 7 ounces)
Cooking spray
4 large eggs

1. Preheat oven to 400°. On a large rimmed baking sheet, toss potatoes and beans with 2 teaspoons olive oil; season with half of the salt and pepper. Roast at 400° for 15 to 20 minutes or until beans are browned and tender. Transfer beans to a plate, toss potatoes again, and continue roasting 10 minutes or until tender. Add potatoes to plate with beans.
2. In a small bowl, whisk together lemon juice, remaining 2 tablespoons olive oil, capers, parsley, and remaining salt and pepper. Divide lettuce among 4 plates; top each with ¼ of the tuna, olives, tomatoes, potatoes, and beans.
3. Spray a large nonstick skillet with cooking spray. Crack two eggs into skillet. Cook until whites are cooked and yolks are just set (about 2 minutes). Repeat with remaining eggs. To serve, drizzle each salad with dressing and place one egg on top.

For nutritional information on this recipe, please turn to the appendix on pages 248–251.

from **Health**

meal maker

PICK A SIDE DISH

• Melon Ball Salad with Lime Syrup, page 185

OR

• crispy breadsticks

ADD A DESSERT

• Flourless Peanut Butter-Chocolate Chip Cookies, page 216

QUICK TIP

Romaine, arugula or Bibb may be substituted for the oak leaf lettuce.

meal maker

PICK A SIDE DISH

- Waldorf Spinach Salad, page 175

OR

- cornbread muffins

ADD A DESSERT

- So Good Brownies, page 220

QUICK TIP

All out of crab? Substitute a pound of peeled cooked shrimp or chopped cooked chicken.

good for company

Corn-and-Crab Chowder

Makes 10 cups ▪ Prep: 30 minutes ▪ Total: 1 hour

---

6 bacon slices
2 celery ribs, diced
1 medium-size green bell pepper, diced
1 medium onion, diced
1 jalapeño pepper, seeded and diced
1 (32-ounce) container chicken broth
3 tablespoons all-purpose flour

3 cups fresh corn kernels (6 ears)
1 pound fresh lump crabmeat, drained and picked
1 cup whipping cream
¼ cup chopped fresh cilantro
½ teaspoon salt
¼ teaspoon pepper
Oyster crackers
Garnish: chopped fresh cilantro

1. Cook bacon in a Dutch oven over medium heat 8 to 10 minutes or until crisp; remove bacon, and drain on paper towels, reserving 2 tablespoons drippings in Dutch oven. Crumble bacon.

2. Sauté celery and next 3 ingredients in hot drippings 5 to 6 minutes or until tender.

3. Whisk together broth and flour until smooth. Add to celery mixture. Stir in corn. Bring to a boil; reduce heat, and simmer, stirring occasionally, 30 minutes. Gently stir in crabmeat and next 4 ingredients; cook 4 to 5 minutes or until thoroughly heated. Serve warm with crumbled bacon and oyster crackers. Garnish, if desired.

from Southern Living

SCAN THIS PHOTO
to see and save
the shopping list.

SCAN THIS PHOTO
to see and save
the shopping list.

quick + easy

Crab Cakes with Spicy Rémoulade

Makes 4 servings ▪ Prep: 25 minutes ▪ Total: 25 minutes

Crab cakes:
1 pound jumbo lump crabmeat, shell pieces removed
2 tablespoons finely chopped green bell pepper
1½ tablespoons canola mayonnaise
¼ teaspoon black pepper
2 green onions, finely chopped
1 large egg, lightly beaten
1 cup panko, divided
2 tablespoons canola oil, divided

Rémoulade:
¼ cup canola mayonnaise
2 teaspoons minced shallots
1 teaspoon chopped fresh tarragon
1 teaspoon chopped fresh parsley
1½ teaspoons Dijon mustard
¾ teaspoon capers, chopped
¾ teaspoon white wine vinegar
¼ teaspoon ground red pepper
Mixed greens (optional)

1. To prepare crab cakes, drain crabmeat on several layers of paper towels. Combine crabmeat, bell pepper, and the next 4 ingredients (through egg), tossing gently. Stir in ¼ cup panko. Place remaining ¾ cup panko in a shallow dish.

2. Divide crab mixture into 8 equal portions. Shape 4 portions into ¾-inch-thick patties; dredge in panko. Heat a large nonstick skillet over medium-high heat. Add 1 tablespoon oil. Add dredged patties; cook 3 minutes on each side or until golden. Remove from pan. Repeat procedure with the remaining crab mixture, panko, and oil.

3. To prepare rémoulade, combine ¼ cup mayonnaise and next 7 ingredients (through red pepper); serve with crab cakes and, if desired, mixed greens.

For nutritional information on this recipe, please turn to the appendix on pages 248–251.

from Cooking Light

meal maker

PICK A SIDE DISH

- Arugula Avocado Salad, page 154

OR

- fresh berries

ADD A DESSERT

- Brown Sugar–Cinnamon Peach Pie, page 238

fish & shellfish

meal maker

PICK A SIDE DISH

- Summer Squash Ribbons with Lemon and Parmesan, page 177

OR

- sautéed spinach

ADD A DESSERT

- Strawberry-Rhubarb Ice Cream, page 246

QUICK TIP

The secret to good risotto? Adding liquid a little at a time and using Arborio rice. The fat grains plump and release starch as they cook, creating a silky, creamy sauce.

healthy choice

Simple Lobster Risotto

Makes 4 servings ▪ Prep: 50 minutes ▪ Total: 1 hour, 10 minutes

---

4 cups fat-free, lower-sodium chicken broth
3 (5-ounce) American lobster tails
3 tablespoons butter, divided
1 cup uncooked Arborio rice or other medium-grain rice
¾ cup frozen green peas, thawed

1. Bring broth and 1½ cups water to a boil in a saucepan. Add lobster; cover and cook for 4 minutes. Remove lobster from pan; cool for 5 minutes. Remove meat from cooked lobster tails, reserving shells. Chop meat. Place shells in a large zip-top plastic bag. Coarsely crush shells using a meat mallet or heavy skillet. Return crushed shells to the broth mixture. Reduce heat to medium-low. Cover and cook for 20 minutes. Strain shell mixture through a sieve over a bowl, reserving broth; discard solids. Return broth mixture to saucepan; keep warm over low heat.

2. Heat 1 tablespoon butter in a medium saucepan over medium-high heat. Add rice to pan; cook 2 minutes, stirring constantly. Stir in 1 cup broth mixture, and cook for 5 minutes or until liquid is nearly absorbed, stirring constantly. Reserve 2 tablespoons broth mixture. Add the remaining broth mixture, ½ cup at a time, stirring constantly until each portion is absorbed before adding the next (about 22 minutes total). Remove from heat, and stir in lobster, the reserved 2 tablespoons broth mixture, 2 tablespoons butter, and green peas.

For nutritional information on this recipe, please turn to the appendix on pages 248–251.

from Cooking Light

SCAN THIS PHOTO to see and save the shopping list.

SCAN THIS PHOTO
to see and save
the shopping list.

Mussels with Red Pepper and Chorizo

Makes 4 servings ▪ Prep: 30 minutes ▪ Total: 30 minutes

2 tablespoons olive oil
1 (3½-ounce) cured chorizo
  sausage, casing removed,
  chopped
1 small red bell pepper, cut into
  thin, short strips
1 small onion, halved and thinly
  sliced
2 garlic cloves, minced

1½ cups dry white wine
1 teaspoon paprika
¼ teaspoon salt
2 pounds fresh mussels, scrubbed
  and debearded
2 tablespoons chopped fresh
  cilantro
Lime wedges

1. Heat olive oil in a large, deep skillet over medium heat. Add chorizo, and sauté 3 minutes or until lightly browned. Add bell pepper, onion, and garlic, and sauté 5 minutes. Add wine, paprika, and salt; bring to a boil. Cover, reduce heat to low, and simmer 5 minutes or until vegetables are tender.

2. Increase heat to medium-high, and add mussels. Cover and cook 2 minutes or until mussels open. Discard any that do not open. Stir in cilantro. Spoon mussels, sauce, and vegetables into 4 shallow serving bowls. Serve immediately with lime wedges.

from COASTAL LIVING

meal maker

PICK A SIDE DISH

- Herbed Couscous Pilaf, page 196

OR

- crusty French bread

ADD A DESSERT

- Tart Lemon Ice with Crushed Strawberries, page 244

fish & shellfish

meal maker

PICK A SIDE DISH

- Steamed Carrots with Garlic-Ginger Butter, page 163

OR

- roasted potato wedges

ADD A DESSERT

- Cherry-Almond Crisp, page 227

healthy choice

Seared Scallops with Bacon, Cabbage, and Apple

Makes 4 servings ▪ Prep: 15 minutes ▪ Total: 25 minutes

3 center-cut bacon slices, cut crosswise into ½-inch pieces
6 cups thinly sliced green cabbage
1 tablespoon chopped fresh thyme
½ cup water
1½ cups chopped Fuji apple (1 medium)

3 tablespoons cider vinegar
½ teaspoon freshly ground black pepper, divided
1 tablespoon canola oil
16 large sea scallops (about 1 pound)
¼ teaspoon salt
2 teaspoons chopped fresh dill

1. Cook bacon in a Dutch oven over medium-high heat until crisp. Remove bacon pieces from pan, reserving 1½ tablespoons drippings in pan. Add sliced cabbage and chopped thyme to pan; sauté 2 minutes, stirring cabbage mixture occasionally. Add ½ cup water, scraping pan to loosen browned bits. Bring mixture to a boil. Reduce heat to medium; cover pan. Cook 5 more minutes. Stir in apple and cider vinegar; cover. Cook 5 minutes. Stir in cooked bacon and ¼ teaspoon pepper.
2. Heat a large, heavy skillet over high heat. Add oil to pan; swirl to coat. Sprinkle scallops with ¼ teaspoon salt and remaining ¼ teaspoon pepper. Add scallops to pan; cook 3 minutes on each side or until scallops are done. Place about 1 cup cabbage mixture on each of 4 plates. Arrange 4 scallops on each serving. Sprinkle each serving with ½ teaspoon dill.

For nutritional information on this recipe, please turn to the appendix on pages 248–251.

from CookingLight

QUICK TIP

Substitute pork tenderloin or boneless chops for the scallops in this simple and quick recipe.

SCAN THIS PHOTO
to see and save
the shopping list.

Scallops with Capers and Brown Butter Sauce

Makes 2 servings ■ Prep: 20 minutes ■ Total: 20 minutes

1 pound sea scallops	¼ cup butter, divided
½ teaspoon salt	1 garlic clove, minced
¼ teaspoon freshly ground black pepper	2 tablespoons fresh lemon juice
	1 tablespoon capers, drained

1. Pat scallops dry, and sprinkle with salt and pepper. Melt 1 tablespoon butter in a large, heavy skillet over high heat. Add scallops, and sear about 2 minutes on each side. Transfer scallops to serving plates, cover, and keep warm.

2. Melt remaining 3 tablespoons butter in skillet. Add garlic; cook 1 minute or until butter begins to turn golden brown. (Be careful not to burn the garlic.) Remove skillet from heat; stir in lemon juice and capers. Spoon sauce over scallops, and serve.

from COASTAL LIVING

healthy choice

Spicy Shrimp Noodle Soup

Makes 4 servings ▪ Prep: 10 minutes ▪ Total: 35 minutes

---

3 cups unsalted beef stock (such as Swanson)

1 cup water

1 tablespoon minced garlic

1 tablespoon sambal oelek (ground fresh chile paste) or ½ teaspoon crushed red pepper

1 teaspoon fish sauce

1 teaspoon lower-sodium soy sauce

2 (3-inch) cinnamon sticks

1 (8-ounce) bottle clam juice

1 ounce dried shiitake mushroom caps, chopped

1 (1-inch) piece peeled fresh ginger

1 star anise

1 pound large shrimp, peeled and deveined

4 ounces uncooked flat rice noodles

½ cup fresh bean sprouts

½ cup diagonally cut green onions

¼ cup fresh cilantro leaves

12 small fresh basil leaves

4 lime wedges

1. Combine first 11 ingredients in a large saucepan. Bring to a boil; reduce heat, and simmer until reduced to 3½ cups (about 12 minutes). Add shrimp; cook 4 minutes or until done. Remove cinnamon, anise, and ginger; discard. Cook rice noodles according to package directions; drain. Place ½ cup noodles in each of 4 bowls, and top each serving with 1 cup stock mixture and about 5 shrimp. Sprinkle evenly with bean sprouts, green onions, cilantro, and basil. Serve with lime wedges.

For nutritional information on this recipe, please turn to the appendix on pages 248–251.

from CookingLight

meal maker

PICK A SIDE DISH

- Lemon-Garlic Swiss Chard, page 178

OR

- steamed carrots

ADD A DESSERT

- Honeyed Apples with Ice Cream, page 223

SCAN THIS PHOTO to see and save the shopping list.

quick + easy

Shrimp Scampi Linguine

Makes 4 servings ▪ Prep: 25 minutes ▪ Total: 25 minutes

8 ounces linguine
3 tablespoons extra-virgin olive oil, divided
1 pound large shrimp, peeled and deveined
6 tablespoons unsalted butter
6 garlic cloves, minced
¼ teaspoon dried crushed red pepper
¼ cup coarsely chopped fresh parsley
2 teaspoons lemon zest
1 tablespoon fresh lemon juice
¾ teaspoon salt

1. Cook pasta in boiling salted water according to package directions; drain.

2. Heat 1 tablespoon oil in a large nonstick skillet over medium-high heat. Add half of shrimp, and cook 1 minute on each side or until opaque. Transfer shrimp to a plate, cover, and keep warm. Repeat with 1 tablespoon oil and remaining shrimp.

3. Melt butter over medium heat in same skillet. Add remaining 1 tablespoon oil, garlic, and red pepper; sauté 3 minutes or until garlic starts to brown. Stir in cooked shrimp, parsley, lemon zest and juice, and salt; cook 1 minute. Add pasta, and cook 1 minute or until hot, tossing constantly. Serve immediately.

from COASTAL LIVING

meal maker

PICK A SIDE DISH

- Garlic-Roasted Kale, page 174

OR

- sautéed grape tomatoes

ADD A DESSERT

- Key Lime Ice Cream Pie, page 243

QUICK TIP

To make it even faster, use fresh linguine instead of dried pasta.

SCAN THIS PHOTO
to see and save
the shopping list.

Mango Avocado Shrimp Salad

Makes 6 servings ▪ Prep: 20 minutes ▪ Total: 20 minutes

3 tablespoons fresh lime juice
2 tablespoons grapeseed or vegetable oil
1 tablespoon sugar
2 large firm-ripe mangoes (2 pounds total)
2 medium firm-ripe avocados (1 pound total)

⅔ cup thinly sliced green onion
⅔ cup chopped fresh cilantro
1 tablespoon minced fresh hot red or green chile (or ½ teaspoon dried red chile flakes)
1 pound (70 to 110 per pound) peeled cooked shrimp

1. In a large bowl, whisk together lime juice, oil, and sugar until sugar dissolves.

2. Dice mangoes and avocados into ¾-inch cubes; add to bowl. Add green onion, cilantro, chile, and shrimp. Mix gently. Serve or cover and chill for up to 1 hour.

For nutritional information on this recipe, please turn to the appendix on pages 248–251.

from *Sunset*

meal maker

PICK A SIDE DISH

• Three-Bean Salad, page 188

OR

• sliced watermelon

ADD A DESSERT

• Luscious Lemon Bars, page 217

QUICK TIP

Maximize the amount of juice you get from a fresh lime by rolling it on the countertop before slicing.

TOFU STEAKS WITH SHIITAKES
AND VEGGIES, *page 147*

SCAN THIS PHOTO
to see and save
the shopping list.

meatless mains

Whether you're interested in trying a meat-free meal once a week or are a seasoned vegetarian, these plant-based dishes are nutritious, balanced, and packed with flavor.

- Marinated Greek-Style Pasta, page 198

OR

- diced tomatoes and cucumbers tossed in Greek salad dressing

ADD A DESSERT

- Flourless Peanut Butter-Chocolate Chip Cookies, page 216

QUICK TIP

Double the grilled veggies so you have some on-hand to top salads, stir into pasta, or add to lasagna or pizza.

quick + easy

Grilled Veggie and Hummus Wraps

Makes 4 servings ▪ Prep: 20 minutes ▪ Total: 20 minutes

4 (½-inch-thick) slices red onion
1 red bell pepper, seeded and quartered
1 (12-ounce) eggplant, cut into ½-inch-thick slices
2 tablespoons olive oil, divided
¼ cup chopped fresh flat-leaf parsley
⅛ teaspoon kosher salt
1 (8-ounce) container plain hummus
4 (1.9-ounce) whole-grain flatbreads (such as Flatout Light)
½ cup crumbled feta cheese

1. Heat a large grill pan over medium-high heat. Brush onion, bell pepper, and eggplant with 1 tablespoon oil. Add onion and bell pepper to pan; cook 3 minutes on each side or until grill marks appear. Remove from pan. Add eggplant to pan; cook 3 minutes on each side or until grill marks appear. Remove from pan; coarsely chop vegetables. Combine vegetables, remaining 1 tablespoon oil, parsley, and salt; toss to combine.

2. Spread ¼ cup hummus over each flatbread, leaving a ½-inch border around edges. Divide vegetables over each flatbread; top each serving with 2 tablespoons cheese. Roll up wraps, and cut diagonally in half.

For nutritional information on this recipe, please turn to the appendix on pages 248–251.

from Cooking Light

quick + easy

Eggplant Parmesan Pizza

Makes 5 servings ▪ Prep: 15 minutes ▪ Total: 30 minutes

1 (1-pound) whole wheat or regular refrigerated pizza dough
Olive oil-flavored cooking spray
2 tablespoons cornmeal
¾ cup marinara sauce
2½ ounces shredded part-skim
   mozzarella cheese (about ¾
   cup)
½ cup part-skim ricotta cheese
3 plum tomatoes, sliced
1 (12-ounce) eggplant, sliced and
   broiled
1 tablespoon finely grated
   Parmesan cheese
Fresh basil leaves

1. Preheat oven to 450°.
2. Roll out pizza dough on a lightly floured surface with a floured rolling pin into a 13-inch round or 13- x 12-inch rectangle. Lightly spray a large baking sheet with olive oil-flavored cooking spray; sprinkle with cornmeal. Transfer dough to prepared sheet. Roll up sides 1 inch to form a rim.
3. Spread marinara sauce on prepared dough and sprinkle with mozzarella cheese. Dollop ricotta cheese over pizza, and top with tomatoes and eggplant. Sprinkle with Parmesan cheese, and bake at 450° for 10 to 12 minutes or until golden brown. Sprinkle with basil leaves, cut into 5 slices, and serve.

For nutritional information on this recipe, please turn to the appendix on pages 248–251.

from **Health**

meal maker

PICK A SIDE DISH

• Three-Bean Salad,
  page 188

OR

• spinach salad

ADD A DESSERT

• Mini Berry Cobblers,
  page 224

meatless mains

QUICK TIP

You can purchase refrigerated pizza dough at your
local pizzeria or supermarket. Let the dough stand
on a floured surface for 15
to 30 minutes to come to
room temperature, allowing
it to be more pliable and
stretchy.

healthy choice

Grilled Stuffed Portobello Mushrooms

Makes 2 servings ▪ Prep: 5 minutes ▪ Total: 15 minutes

---

2 (4½-inch) portobello mushroom caps
2 teaspoons olive oil, divided
1 garlic clove, minced
¾ cup minced onion (1 small)
1½ teaspoons chopped fresh oregano

½ cup bagged baby spinach leaves
¼ cup grated Parmesan cheese
⅓ cup Italian-seasoned panko (Japanese breadcrumbs)
1½ teaspoons balsamic vinegar
½ teaspoon black pepper

1. Prepare grill.

2. Remove brown gills from undersides of mushrooms using a spoon; discard gills. Set mushroom caps aside.

3. Heat 1 teaspoon oil in a large nonstick skillet over medium-high heat. Add garlic and onion; sauté 2 minutes. Add oregano and spinach; sauté 1 minute or until spinach wilts.

4. Transfer spinach mixture to a medium bowl; stir in remaining 1 teaspoon oil, cheese, panko, vinegar, and pepper. Divide filling evenly between mushrooms, spooning onto gill sides.

5. Grill 7 minutes. Serve immediately.

For nutritional information on this recipe, please turn to the appendix on pages 248–251.

from Oxmoor House.

meal maker

PICK A SIDE DISH

- Creamy Cannellini Beans with Garlic and Oregano, page 191

OR

- grilled tomatoes

ADD A DESSERT

- Peanut Butter Ice Cream Sandwiches, page 247

meatless mains

QUICK TIP

This recipe makes 2 servings but can easily be doubled or tripled to feed a crowd.

meal maker

PICK A SIDE DISH

- Bulgur Wheat Salad with Tomato and Eggplant, page 193

OR

- fruit salad

ADD A DESSERT

- White and Dark Chocolate Pudding Parfaits, page 237

great for company

Spinach Pie with Goat Cheese, Raisins, and Pine Nuts

Makes 8 servings ▪ Prep: 20 minutes ▪ Total: 2 hours

⅓ cup olive oil, divided
2 cups minced onion (about 1 large)
5 (9-ounce) packages fresh spinach
½ cup golden raisins
2 cups (8 ounces) crumbled goat cheese

⅓ cup pine nuts, toasted
½ teaspoon kosher salt
¼ teaspoon ground black pepper
12 sheets frozen phyllo dough, thawed
Cooking spray

1. Preheat oven to 400°.

2. Heat 3 tablespoons oil in a large Dutch oven over medium heat. Add onion to pan; cook 5 minutes or until browned, stirring occasionally. Add spinach, 1 package at a time; cook 3 minutes or until spinach wilts, stirring frequently. Simmer spinach mixture 40 minutes or until liquid evaporates. Stir in raisins. Remove from heat; cool completely. Stir in cheese, nuts, salt, and pepper.

3. Press 1 phyllo sheet into bottom and up sides of a 13 x 9–inch baking dish coated with cooking spray (cover remaining dough to keep from drying); lightly coat phyllo with cooking spray. Repeat procedure with 7 phyllo sheets. Spread spinach mixture in an even layer onto phyllo. Place 1 phyllo sheet on a large cutting board or work surface (cover remaining dough to keep from drying); lightly brush with 1½ teaspoons oil. Repeat procedure with the remaining 3 phyllo sheets and the remaining 1½ tablespoons oil. Place phyllo layer over spinach mixture; tuck in sides to enclose spinach fully. Bake at 400° for 30 minutes. Remove from oven; let stand 15 minutes.

For nutritional information on this recipe, please turn to the appendix on pages 248–251.

from CookingLight

SCAN THIS PHOTO
to see and save
the shopping list.

meatless mains

- Everyday Roast Vegetables, page 181

OR

- Caesar salad

ADD A DESSERT

- Key Lime Ice Cream Pie, page 243

quick + easy

Fresh Tomato Basil Pizza

Makes 8 servings ▪ Prep: 15 minutes ▪ Total: 30 minutes

**1 (1-pound) package refrigerated
pizza dough**
2 or 3 garlic cloves, thinly sliced
**About ¼ teaspoon flaked sea
salt, divided**

**2 to 3 tablespoons extra-virgin
olive oil**
**10 to 12 small tomatoes, halved
or quartered**
6 or 7 basil leaves, torn

1. Preheat oven to 500° with a pizza stone on the bottom rack.
2. Roll out pizza dough on a floured pizza peel or upside-down large baking sheet. Press garlic slices into surface of dough and season with a pinch of salt. Slide pizza from peel onto hot pizza stone in oven.
3. Bake pizza at 500° until puffed, blistered, and browned, 10 to 12 minutes. Remove from oven, drizzle liberally with oil, and top with tomatoes and basil. Sprinkle with remaining pinch of salt.

from **Sunset**

SCAN THIS PHOTO to see and save the shopping list.

SCAN THIS PHOTO to see and save the shopping list.

Lentil-Barley Burgers with Fiery Fruit Salsa

Makes 4 servings ▪ Prep: 35 minutes ▪ Total: 2 hours

Salsa:
¼ cup finely chopped pineapple
¼ cup finely chopped mango
¼ cup finely chopped tomatillo
¼ cup halved grape tomatoes
1 tablespoon fresh lime juice
1 serrano chile, minced

Burgers:
1½ cups water
½ cup dried lentils
Cooking spray
1 cup chopped onion
¼ cup grated carrot
2 teaspoons minced garlic
2 tablespoons tomato paste

1½ teaspoons ground cumin
¾ teaspoon dried oregano
½ teaspoon chili powder
¾ teaspoon salt
¾ cup cooked pearl barley
½ cup panko (Japanese bread-crumbs)
¼ cup finely chopped fresh parsley
½ teaspoon coarsely ground black pepper
2 large egg whites
1 large egg
3 tablespoons canola oil, divided

1. To prepare salsa, combine first 6 ingredients; cover and refrigerate.

2. To prepare burgers, combine 1½ cups water and lentils in a saucepan; bring to a boil. Cover, reduce heat, and simmer 25 minutes or until lentils are tender. Drain. Place half of lentils in a large bowl. Place remaining lentils in a food processor; process until smooth. Add processed lentils to whole lentils in bowl.

3. Heat a large nonstick skillet over medium-high heat. Coat pan with cooking spray. Add onion and carrot; sauté 6 minutes or until tender, stirring occasionally. Add garlic; cook 1 minute, stirring constantly. Add tomato paste, cumin, oregano, chili powder, and ¼ teaspoon salt; cook 1 minute, stirring constantly. Add onion mixture to lentils. Add remaining ½ teaspoon salt, barley, and next 5 ingredients (through egg); stir well. Cover and refrigerate 1 hour or until firm.

4. Divide mixture into 8 portions, shaping each into a ½-inch-thick patty. Heat 1½ tablespoons oil in a large nonstick skillet over medium-high heat. Add 4 patties; cook 3 minutes on each side or until browned. Repeat procedure with remaining 1½ tablespoons oil and 4 patties. Serve with salsa.

For nutritional information on this recipe, please turn to the appendix on pages 248–251.

from CookingLight

meal maker

PICK A SIDE DISH

• Home Fries, page 204

OR

• roasted sweet potato wedges

ADD A DESSERT

• Cherry-Almond Crisp, page 227

meatless mains

QUICK TIP

Use leftover cooked pearl barley with lentils, veggies, and seasonings for a main-dish burger sans the bun.

meal maker

PICK A SIDE DISH

- Buttery Lemon Broccolini, page 160

OR

- fruit kebabs

ADD A DESSERT

- Key Lime Ice Cream Pie, page 243

QUICK TIP

To save time, don't seed the tomato and cucumber. Just dice them.

Red Quinoa Salad

Makes 4 servings ▪ Prep: 10 minutes ▪ Total: 1 hour, 20 minutes

1 cup uncooked red quinoa
⅓ cup olive oil
2 tablespoons red wine vinegar
1½ teaspoons finely minced shallots
¼ teaspoon kosher salt
¼ teaspoon freshly ground black pepper
2 cups (½-inch) diced seeded tomato
½ cup (½-inch) diced seeded cucumber
3 tablespoons chopped fresh mint
1 tablespoon chopped fresh oregano
1 (15-ounce) can chickpeas (garbanzo beans), rinsed and drained
2 ounces crumbled feta cheese (about ½ cup)
4 lemon wedges

1. Cook quinoa according to package directions, omitting salt and fat. Drain and place in a large bowl. Let cool 1 hour.
2. While quinoa cools, combine oil and next 4 ingredients (through pepper) in a small bowl, stirring with a whisk. Let stand 20 minutes.
3. Add dressing, tomato, and next 4 ingredients (through chickpeas) to quinoa; toss well. Add cheese, and toss gently. Serve with lemon wedges.

For nutritional information on this recipe, please turn to the appendix on pages 248–251.

from Oxmoor House.

SCAN THIS PHOTO to see and save the shopping list.

meal maker

PICK A SIDE DISH

- Steamed Carrots with Garlic-Ginger Butter, page 163

OR

- mixed green salad

ADD A DESSERT

- Strawberry-Rhubarb Ice Cream, page 246

quick + easy

Creamy Spring Pasta

Makes 4 servings ▪ Prep: 15 minutes ▪ Total: 30 minutes

3 quarts water
2 ounces French bread baguette, torn into pieces
1 tablespoon butter
3 garlic cloves, minced and divided
1½ cups (2-inch) diagonally cut asparagus
1 cup frozen green peas
6 ounces uncooked fettuccine
2 teaspoons olive oil
⅓ cup finely chopped sweet onion

1 tablespoon all-purpose flour
¼ cup fat-free, lower-sodium vegetable or chicken broth
1 cup 1% low-fat milk
3 ounces ⅓-less-fat cream cheese
1 ounce Parmigiano-Reggiano cheese, grated (about ¼ cup packed)
½ teaspoon kosher salt
¼ teaspoon freshly ground black pepper
2 tablespoons chopped fresh tarragon

1. Bring 3 quarts water to a boil in a Dutch oven.
2. Place torn bread in a food processor; process until coarse crumbs form. Melt butter in a large skillet over medium-high heat. Add 1 garlic clove to pan; sauté 1 minute. Add breadcrumbs; sauté 3 minutes or until golden brown and toasted. Remove breadcrumb mixture from pan; wipe pan clean with paper towels.
3. Add asparagus and peas to boiling water; cook for 3 minutes or until crisp-tender. Remove from pan with a slotted spoon. Rinse under cold water; drain.
4. Add pasta to boiling water; cook 10 minutes or until al dente. Drain and keep warm.
5. Heat olive oil in skillet over medium heat. Add onion and the remaining 2 garlic cloves; cook for 3 minutes or until tender, stirring frequently. Place flour in a small bowl; gradually whisk in broth. Add broth mixture and milk to pan, stirring constantly with a whisk; bring to a boil. Reduce heat; cook 1 minute or until thickened. Remove from heat; add cheeses, salt, and pepper, stirring until cheeses melt. Add pasta, asparagus, and peas; toss well. Sprinkle with breadcrumbs and tarragon.

For nutritional information on this recipe, please turn to the appendix on pages 248–251.

from CookingLight

SCAN THIS PHOTO to see and save the shopping list.

meal maker

PICK A SIDE DISH

- Buttery Lemon Broccolini, page 160

OR

- sautéed spinach

ADD A DESSERT

- Luscious Lemon Bars, page 217

quick + easy

Tortellini with Peas and Tarragon

Makes 4 servings ▪ Prep: 15 minutes ▪ Total: 20 minutes

---

1 pound frozen cheese tortellini
2 tablespoons olive oil
1 onion, chopped
3 tablespoons unsalted butter
2 cloves garlic, finely chopped
1½ cups frozen peas

½ teaspoon kosher salt
¼ teaspoon pepper
2 tablespoons chopped fresh tarragon
½ cup grated Parmesan cheese

1. Cook tortellini according to package directions.
2. Meanwhile, heat oil in a large skillet over medium heat. Add onion and cook until soft, about 6 minutes. Increase heat to medium-high. Add the butter and cook until it turns golden brown, about 3 minutes. Stir in the garlic, peas, salt, and pepper and cook until heated through, 2 to 3 minutes. Add the tortellini, tarragon, and half the Parmesan and toss.
3. Divide among bowls and sprinkle with the remaining Parmesan.

For nutritional information on this recipe, please turn to the appendix on pages 248–251.

from REALSIMPLE

meal maker

PICK A SIDE DISH

- Mozzarella, Tomato, and Basil Salad, page 179

OR

- steamed sugar snap peas

ADD A DESSERT

- Free-form Strawberry Cheesecake, page 229

healthy choice

Browned Butter Gnocchi with Broccoli and Nuts

Makes 6 servings ▪ Prep: 10 minutes ▪ Total: 25 minutes

2 (16-ounce) packages prepared gnocchi
5 cups chopped broccoli florets
2 tablespoons unsalted butter
2 tablespoons extra-virgin olive oil

¼ teaspoon freshly ground black pepper
3 tablespoons pine nuts, toasted
1.5 ounces shaved fresh Pecorino Romano cheese (about ⅓ cup)

1. Cook gnocchi in a large Dutch oven according to package directions. Add broccoli during last minute of cooking; cook 1 minute. Drain.
2. Heat a large skillet over medium heat. Add butter and oil; cook 7 minutes or until butter browns. Add gnocchi mixture and pepper to pan; toss to coat. Spoon about 1½ cups gnocchi mixture into each of 6 shallow bowls. Sprinkle each serving with 1½ teaspoons pine nuts and about 2 teaspoons cheese.

For nutritional information on this recipe, please turn to the appendix on pages 248–251.

from CookingLight

QUICK TIP

Look for shelf-stable packaged gnocchi with the dried pasta. To cut costs, swap chopped almonds or pecans for pine nuts.

- Grilled Zucchini with Sea Salt, page 182

OR

- roasted green beans

ADD A DESSERT

- Chocolate-Caramel Pecan Pie, page 240

QUICK TIP

For maximum creaminess and meltability, grate your own cheese and forego the preshredded cheese, which is drier.

great for company

Creamy Four-Cheese Macaroni

Makes 8 servings ▪ Prep: 25 minutes ▪ Total: 1 hour

1.5 ounces all-purpose flour (about ⅓ cup)
2⅔ cups 1% low-fat milk
2 ounces shredded fontina cheese (about ½ cup)
2 ounces grated Parmesan cheese (about ½ cup)
2 ounces shredded extra-sharp cheddar cheese (about ½ cup)
3 ounces light processed cheese (such as light Velveeta)

6 cups cooked elbow macaroni (about 3 cups uncooked)
½ teaspoon salt
¼ teaspoon freshly ground black pepper
Cooking spray
⅓ cup crushed melba toasts (about 12 pieces)
1 tablespoon canola oil
1 garlic clove, minced

1. Preheat oven to 375°.
2. Weigh or lightly spoon flour into a dry measuring cup; level with a knife. Place flour in a large saucepan. Gradually add milk, stirring with a whisk until blended. Cook over medium heat until thick (about 8 minutes), stirring constantly with a whisk. Remove from heat; let stand 4 minutes or until sauce cools to 155°. Add cheeses, and stir until the cheeses melt. Stir in cooked macaroni, salt, and black pepper.
3. Spoon mixture into a 2-quart glass or ceramic baking dish coated with cooking spray. Combine crushed toasts, oil, and garlic in small bowl; stir until well blended. Sprinkle over macaroni mixture. Bake at 375° for 30 minutes or until bubbly.

For nutritional information on this recipe, please turn to the appendix on pages 248–251.

from CookingLight

SCAN THIS PHOTO
to see and save
the shopping list.

SCAN THIS PHOTO to see and save the shopping list.

healthy choice

Chickpeas in Curried Coconut Broth

Makes 6 servings ▪ Prep: 10 minutes ▪ Total: 6 hours, 15 minutes

2 teaspoons canola oil
1½ cups chopped onion
2 garlic cloves, minced
2 (19-ounce) cans chickpeas (garbanzo beans), drained and rinsed
2 (14.5-ounce) cans no-salt-added diced tomatoes, undrained

1 (13.5-ounce) can light coconut milk
1 tablespoon curry powder
2 tablespoons chopped pickled jalapeño pepper
1 teaspoon salt
½ cup chopped fresh cilantro
6 cups hot cooked basmati rice

1. Heat a large nonstick skillet over medium heat. Add oil to pan; swirl to coat. Add onion and garlic; sauté 5 minutes or until onion is tender.
2. Place onion mixture, chickpeas, and next 5 ingredients (through salt) in a 3½-quart electric slow cooker; stir well. Cover and cook on LOW for 6 to 8 hours. Stir in cilantro. Serve over rice.

For nutritional information on this recipe, please turn to the appendix on pages 248–251.

from Oxmoor House.

meal maker

PICK A SIDE DISH

• Lavender-Scented Summer Fruit Salad, page 183

OR

• steamed broccoli

ADD A DESSERT

• Roasted Banana Bars with Browned Butter–Pecan Frosting, page 219

meatless mains

QUICK TIP

Use a pouch of microwave basmati rice instead. It cooks in just 90 seconds.

meal maker

PICK A SIDE DISH

- Creamy Lime Slaw, page 164

OR

- sliced mango

ADD A DESSERT

- Peanut Butter Ice Cream Sandwiches, page 247

quick + easy

Cheesy Corn-and-Black-Bean Quesadillas

Makes 8 servings ▪ Prep: 25 minutes ▪ Total: 35 minutes

1 (15.5-ounce) can black beans, drained and rinsed
1½ cups frozen corn kernels, thawed
1 tablespoon canola oil
1 small onion, chopped
1 jalapeño, seeded and finely chopped

2 cloves garlic, minced
6 ounces pepper Jack cheese, shredded (1½ cups)
Salt and pepper
8 (8-inch) flour tortillas
Salsa

1. In a bowl, coarsely mash beans with a potato masher. Warm a large skillet over medium-high heat; add corn and cook for 3 to 4 minutes, stirring occasionally, until corn begins to brown. Add corn to bowl with beans.

2. In same skillet, warm oil. Add onion and jalapeño and sauté for 2 minutes. Add garlic and sauté 1 minute longer. Stir mixture into bowl with beans and corn. Let mixture cool to room temperature, about 10 minutes.

3. When cool, stir in cheese and season with salt and pepper. Preheat oven to 200°. Place a tortilla on a work surface and spread a ½-cup portion of bean mixture over half. Fold tortilla in half. Repeat with remaining tortillas and bean mixture. Warm a large skillet over medium-high heat. Cook as many tortillas as fit in skillet, 3 minutes, then flip quesadillas and cook until golden brown and crispy and cheese is melting, 2 to 3 minutes longer. Place quesadillas on a baking sheet and keep warm in oven while you cook remaining quesadillas. Cut into 6 wedges and serve with salsa.

For nutritional information on this recipe, please turn to the appendix on pages 248–251.

from all you

meatless mains

SCAN THIS PHOTO
to see and save
the shopping list.

great for company

Black Beans and Coconut-Lime Rice

Makes 6 servings ▪ Prep: 30 minutes ▪ Total: 50 minutes

1 cup sweetened flaked coconut
1½ cups vegetable or chicken
   broth
¼ teaspoon salt
¼ teaspoon pepper
3 tablespoons butter, divided
1¼ cups uncooked basmati rice
1 small onion, chopped
1 poblano pepper, diced
2 (15-ounce) cans black beans,
   drained and rinsed

2 teaspoons chili powder
1 teaspoon ground cumin
1 lime
2 green onions, thinly sliced
½ cup chopped fresh cilantro
Toppings: diced mango, sliced
   radishes, sliced fresh jalapeño
   peppers, sour cream

1. Preheat oven to 350°. Bake coconut in a single layer on a baking sheet 8 to 10 minutes or until toasted.
2. Bring broth, salt, pepper, 2 tablespoons butter, and 1 cup water to a boil in a 2-quart saucepan. Stir in rice. Cover, reduce heat to low, and cook 15 to 20 minutes or until rice is tender and water is absorbed.
3. Meanwhile, melt remaining 1 tablespoon butter in a medium saucepan over medium-high heat; add onion and poblano pepper, and sauté 5 minutes or until tender. Stir in black beans, chili powder, cumin, and ¾ cup water. Cook over medium-low heat, stirring occasionally, 15 minutes.
4. Grate zest from lime, avoiding pale bitter pith, into a bowl; squeeze juice from lime into bowl.
5. Fluff rice with a fork. Fold lime zest and juice, coconut, green onions, and cilantro into hot cooked rice. Serve bean mixture over rice with desired toppings.

from **Southern Living**

meal maker

PICK A SIDE DISH

- Creamy Lime Slaw, page 164

OR

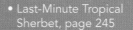

- sautéed grape tomatoes

ADD A DESSERT

- Last-Minute Tropical Sherbet, page 245

meatless mains

meal maker

PICK A SIDE DISH

- Grilled Corn Poblano Salad with Chipotle Vinaigrette, page 169

OR

- melon salad

ADD A DESSERT

- Tart Lemon Ice with Crushed Strawberries, page 244

quick + easy

Mexicali Meatless Tostadas

Makes 6 servings ▪ Prep: 10 minutes ▪ Total: 15 minutes

1 (12-ounce) package frozen meatless burger crumbles
1 tablespoon taco seasoning
12 tostada shells
1 (8.5-ounce) pouch ready-to-serve whole-grain Santa Fe rice
1 (16-ounce) can refried beans
1 (8-ounce) package shredded Mexican four-cheese blend
Pico de gallo and diced avocado
Garnish: fresh cilantro leaves

1. Preheat oven to 425°. Prepare crumbles according to package directions. Stir taco seasoning into hot crumble mixture. Prepare tostada shells and rice according to package directions.

2. Layer refried beans, crumble mixture, and rice on tostada shells. Sprinkle with cheese. Bake at 425° for 5 to 6 minutes or until cheese is melted. Serve with pico de gallo and avocado.

Note: We tested with MorningStar Farms Meal Starters Grillers Recipe Crumbles.

from **Southern Living**

meal maker

PICK A SIDE DISH

- New-Fashioned Apple and Raisin Slaw, page 184

OR

- cucumber salad

ADD A DESSERT

- So Good Brownies, page 220

healthy choice

Gingery Butternut Squash and Tofu Curry

Makes 4 servings ▪ Prep: 15 minutes ▪ Total: 30 minutes

2 teaspoons olive oil
1 (20-ounce) package cubed butternut squash, large pieces cut in half
1 large onion, diced
1 cup curry-style simmer sauce
1 cup 1% low-fat milk
½ cup water
4 ounces cubed firm tofu, patted dry
½ pound (about 1 bunch) Broccolini, trimmed and cut into 1-inch pieces
3 cups cooked jasmine rice
Fresh basil leaves

1. Heat oil in a large saucepan over medium heat; add squash and onion. Cook until vegetables have softened (about 10 minutes), stirring often.
2. Combine simmer sauce, milk, and ½ cup water, whisking well. Place tofu in the saucepan; add simmer sauce mixture. Cover pot; simmer until vegetables are tender (about 7 minutes). Remove lid. Add Broccolini; simmer until tender (about 5 minutes).
3. Place rice in 4 bowls; top with curry and basil.

For nutritional information on this recipe, please turn to the appendix on pages 248–251.

from **Health**

meatless mains

SCAN THIS PHOTO
to see and save
the shopping list.

Veggie and Tofu Stir-Fry

Makes 4 servings ▪ Prep: 20 minutes ▪ Total: 50 minutes

1 (14-ounce) package water-packed extra-firm tofu, drained
1 tablespoon canola oil, divided
¼ teaspoon black pepper
3½ teaspoons cornstarch, divided
3 large green onions, cut into 1-inch pieces
3 garlic cloves, sliced
1 tablespoon julienne-cut ginger
4 small baby bok choy, quartered lengthwise
2 large carrots, peeled and julienne-cut
1 cup snow peas, trimmed
2 tablespoons Shaoxing (Chinese rice wine) or dry sherry
¼ cup organic vegetable broth
2 tablespoons lower-sodium soy sauce
1 tablespoon hoisin sauce
1 teaspoon dark sesame oil

1. Cut tofu lengthwise into 4 equal pieces; cut each piece crosswise into ½-inch squares. Place tofu on several layers of paper towels; cover with additional paper towels. Let stand 30 minutes, pressing down occasionally.

2. Heat a large wok or skillet over high heat. Add 1½ teaspoons canola oil to pan; swirl to coat. Combine tofu, pepper, and 2 teaspoons cornstarch in a medium bowl; toss to coat. Add tofu to pan; stir-fry 8 minutes, turning to brown on all sides. Remove tofu from pan with a slotted spoon; place in a medium bowl. Add onions, garlic, and ginger to pan; stir-fry 1 minute. Remove from pan; add to tofu.

3. Add remaining 1½ teaspoons canola oil to pan; swirl to coat. Add bok choy; stir-fry 3 minutes. Add carrots; stir-fry 2 minutes. Add snow peas; stir-fry 1 minute. Add Shaoxing; cook 30 seconds, stirring constantly. Stir in tofu mixture.

4. Combine remaining 1½ teaspoons cornstarch, broth, and remaining ingredients in a small bowl, stirring with a whisk. Add broth mixture to pan; cook until slightly thickened (about 1 minute).

For nutritional information on this recipe, please turn to the appendix on pages 248–251.

from CookingLight

meatless mains

meal maker

PICK A SIDE DISH

- Brown Rice Pilaf with Almonds and Parsley, page 203

OR

- soba noodles

ADD A DESSERT

- Bittersweet Fudge with Sea Salt, page 222

QUICK TIP

Make sure to thoroughly whisk the cornstarch and broth together before adding it to the stir-fry to prevent the cornstarch from clumping.

SCAN THIS PHOTO
to see and save
the shopping list.

healthy choice

Tofu Steaks with Shiitakes and Veggies

Makes 4 servings ▪ Prep: 20 minutes ▪ Total: 35 minutes

1 (14-ounce) package extra-firm tofu, drained
3 tablespoons dark sesame oil, divided
3 tablespoons lower-sodium soy sauce, divided
1 cup julienne-cut red bell pepper
1 cup matchstick-cut carrots
⅛ teaspoon salt
4 garlic cloves, thinly sliced
1 (5-ounce) package presliced shiitake mushrooms
½ cup organic vegetable broth
1 tablespoon honey
2 teaspoons sherry vinegar
½ teaspoon crushed red pepper
Cooking spray

1. Cut tofu in half crosswise and again in half lengthwise. Pierce tofu liberally with a fork. Place in a shallow dish. Combine 1 tablespoon oil and 1 tablespoon soy sauce in a small bowl. Pour soy mixture over tofu; let stand 15 minutes, turning once. Set aside.

2. Heat a large nonstick skillet over medium-high heat. Add 1 tablespoon oil; swirl to coat. Add bell pepper, carrot, and salt; sauté 3 minutes. Remove from pan. Add remaining 1 tablespoon oil; swirl to coat. Add garlic and mushrooms; sauté 4 minutes. Add remaining 2 tablespoons soy sauce, broth, and next 3 ingredients. Simmer 3 minutes or until thickened. Remove from heat.

3. Remove tofu from marinade; reserve marinade. Heat a grill pan over high heat. Coat pan with cooking spray. Add tofu to pan; cook 3 minutes on each side, basting occasionally with reserved marinade. Arrange 1 tofu steak on each of 4 plates; top each serving with about ⅓ cup carrot mixture and about 2 tablespoons mushroom mixture.

For nutritional information on this recipe, please turn to the appendix on pages 248–251.

from Cooking Light

meal maker

PICK A SIDE DISH

• Edamame Salad, page 192

OR

• basmati rice

ADD A DESSERT

• Honeyed Apples with Ice Cream, page 223

meatless mains

QUICK TIP

Piercing the tofu with a fork allows the sesame oil and soy sauce to soak into the tofu, amping up the flavor.

meal maker

PICK A SIDE DISH

- Simple Sesame Salad, page 156

OR

- steam-in-bag edamame

ADD A DESSERT

- Tart Lemon Ice with Crushed Strawberries, page 244

Lettuce Wraps with Hoisin-Peanut Sauce

Makes 4 servings ▪ Prep: 20 minutes ▪ Total: 40 minutes

Sauce:
1 teaspoon canola oil
1 tablespoon minced shallot
⅓ cup water
2 tablespoons creamy peanut butter
4 teaspoons hoisin sauce
⅛ teaspoon crushed red pepper
1 tablespoon fresh lime juice

Filling:
1 (14-ounce) package extra-firm tofu, drained and crumbled
1 tablespoon dark sesame oil
6 thinly sliced green onions (about ⅔ cup), divided

½ cup plus 2 tablespoons chopped fresh cilantro, divided
3 tablespoons lower-sodium soy sauce
1 teaspoon grated fresh ginger
2 teaspoons sugar
½ teaspoon Sriracha (hot chile sauce, such as Huy Fong)
1 cup matchstick-cut cucumbers
1 cup matchstick-cut carrots
2 cups hot cooked sticky rice
8 Bibb lettuce leaves

1. To prepare sauce, heat a small saucepan over medium heat. Add canola oil to pan; swirl to coat. Add shallot, and sauté for 2 minutes. Add ⅓ cup water and next 3 ingredients (through red pepper), and stir with a whisk. Bring to a boil; cook 1 minute. Remove from heat; stir in lime juice.
2. To prepare filling, spread crumbled tofu in a single layer on several layers of paper towels; cover with additional paper towels. Let stand 20 minutes, pressing down occasionally.
3. Heat a large nonstick skillet over medium-high heat. Add sesame oil to pan; swirl to coat. Add ⅓ cup green onions; sauté 1 minute. Add tofu; sauté for 4 minutes, stirring occasionally. Add 2 tablespoons cilantro, soy sauce, ginger, sugar, and Sriracha; sauté 1 minute. Remove from heat; stir in cucumbers, carrots, and remaining green onions.
4. Spoon ¼ cup rice into each lettuce leaf. Top with about ½ cup tofu mixture; sprinkle with 1 tablespoon cilantro. Serve with sauce.

For nutritional information on this recipe, please turn to the appendix on pages 248–251.

from Cooking Light

SCAN THIS PHOTO
to see and save
the shopping list.

- Quinoa with Roasted Garlic, Tomatoes, and Spinach, page 201

OR

- blanched asparagus with hollandaise

- Real Banana Pudding, page 235

QUICK TIP

Use a mandoline, a V-slicer, or the slicing disk on your food processor to quickly turn zucchini into a pile of superthin slices.

great for company

Zucchini and Caramelized Onion Quiche

Makes 6 servings ▪ Prep: 20 minutes ▪ Total: 2 hours, 20 minutes

½ (14.1-ounce) package refrigerated pie dough
1 tablespoon olive oil
4 cups (⅛-inch-thick) slices zucchini
3 garlic cloves, minced
¾ teaspoon kosher salt, divided
½ cup finely chopped Basic Caramelized Onions

1 cup 1% low-fat milk
1½ tablespoons all-purpose flour
½ teaspoon freshly ground black pepper
3 large eggs
2 ounces Parmigiano-Reggiano cheese, grated (about ½ cup)

1. Preheat oven to 425°.
2. Roll dough into a 12-inch circle. Fit dough into a 10-inch deep-dish pie plate. Fold edges under; flute. Line dough with foil; arrange pie weights or dried beans on foil. Bake at 425° for 12 minutes or until edges are golden. Remove weights and foil; bake an additional 2 minutes. Cool on a wire rack.
3. Reduce oven temperature to 375°.
4. Heat a large nonstick skillet over medium-high heat. Add oil to pan; swirl to coat. Add zucchini and garlic; sprinkle with ¼ teaspoon salt. Sauté 5 minutes or until crisp-tender. Cool slightly.
5. Arrange Basic Caramelized Onions over bottom of crust; top with zucchini mixture. Combine remaining ½ teaspoon salt, milk, flour, pepper, eggs, and cheese in a medium bowl, stirring well with a whisk. Pour milk mixture over zucchini mixture. Bake at 375° for 35 minutes or until set. Let stand 10 minutes before serving.

Basic Caramelized Onions

Makes 8 servings ▪ Prep: 10 minutes ▪ Total: 1 hour, 25 minutes

3 tablespoons olive oil
1 tablespoon butter
12 cups vertically sliced yellow onion

¼ teaspoon kosher salt

1. Heat a large Dutch oven over medium heat. Add oil and butter; swirl until butter melts. Add onion and salt; cook 15 minutes or until onion begins to soften, stirring occasionally. Reduce heat to medium-low. Cook 50 minutes or until very tender, stirring occasionally. Cook an additional 10 minutes or until browned and caramelized, stirring frequently.

For nutritional information on this recipe, please turn to the appendix on pages 248–251.

from Cooking Light

ROASTED BABY BEET SALAD,
page 157

SCAN THIS PHOTO
to see and save
the shopping list.

vegetable sides & salads

Jazz up your main course by pairing it with one of these select, fresh-from-the-garden sides.

meal maker

PICK A MAIN DISH

- Crab Cakes with Spicy Rémoulade, page 103

OR

- Enchilada Casserole, page 48

OR

- slices of rotisserie chicken and toasted tortillas

ADD A DESSERT

- Cherry-Almond Crisp, page 227

quick + easy

Arugula Avocado Salad

Makes 4 servings ▪ Prep: 10 minutes ▪ Total: 10 minutes

¼ cup extra-virgin olive oil
2 tablespoons fresh lemon juice
Salt and freshly ground black pepper
6 ounces arugula leaves
1 avocado, chopped

1 medium tomato, chopped
2 hearts of palm, chopped
⅓ cup pine nuts, toasted
2 tablespoons grated Parmesan cheese

1. In a small bowl, whisk together oil and lemon juice to make dressing. Add salt and pepper to taste. Set aside.

2. In a large salad bowl, combine arugula, avocado, tomato, and hearts of palm. Toss with dressing. Top with pine nuts and cheese.

For nutritional information on this recipe, please turn to the appendix on pages 248–251.

from **Sunset**

healthy choice

Grilled Asparagus with Caper Vinaigrette

Makes 6 servings ▪ Prep: 20 minutes ▪ Total: 20 minutes

1½ pounds asparagus spears, trimmed
3 tablespoons extra-virgin olive oil, divided
½ teaspoon kosher salt, divided
Cooking spray
1 tablespoon red wine vinegar

½ teaspoon Dijon mustard
¼ teaspoon freshly ground black pepper
1 garlic clove, minced
2 teaspoons capers, coarsely chopped
¼ cup small basil leaves

1. Preheat grill to medium-high heat.
2. Place asparagus in a shallow dish. Add 1 tablespoon oil and ¼ teaspoon salt, tossing well to coat. Place asparagus on grill rack coated with cooking spray; grill 4 minutes or until crisp-tender, turning after 2 minutes.
3. Combine remaining ¼ teaspoon salt, vinegar, and next 3 ingredients (through garlic); stir with a whisk. Slowly pour remaining 2 tablespoons oil into vinegar mixture, stirring constantly with a whisk. Stir in capers. Arrange asparagus on a serving platter; drizzle with vinaigrette, and sprinkle with basil.

For nutritional information on this recipe, please turn to the appendix on pages 248–251.

from CookingLight

meal maker

PICK A MAIN DISH

- Grilled Pork Chops with Two-Melon Salsa, page 59

OR

- Cedar Plank-Grilled Salmon with Mango Kiwi Salsa, page 94

ADD A DESSERT

- Grilled Pound Cake with Lemon Cream and Blueberries, page 232

vegetable sides & salads

meal maker

PICK A MAIN DISH

- Coconut-Curry Chicken Soup, page 16

OR

- Stir-Fried Beef with Noodles, page 54

OR

- Lettuce Wraps with Hoisin-Peanut Sauce, page 148

ADD A DESSERT

- Luscious Lemon Bars, page 217

healthy choice

Simple Sesame Salad

Makes 4 servings ▪ Prep: 10 minutes ▪ Total: 10 minutes

1½ tablespoons roasted ground sesame seeds

1 tablespoon coarsely ground Korean chile (gochugaru)

1½ tablespoons dark sesame oil

1½ tablespoons rice vinegar

1½ teaspoons lower-sodium soy sauce

¼ teaspoon kosher salt

6 cups torn romaine lettuce

⅓ cup slivered red onion

1. Combine first 6 ingredients in a large bowl, stirring with a whisk. Add lettuce and onion; toss to coat. Serve immediately.

For nutritional information on this recipe, please turn to the appendix on pages 248–251.

from CookingLight

QUICK TIP

Can't find roasted ground sesame seeds? Make your own. Simply toast sesame seeds in a dry skillet until deeply golden, allow them to cool, and crush with a mortar and pestle.

great for company

Roasted Baby Beet Salad

Makes 6 servings ▪ Prep: 15 minutes ▪ Total: 1 hour, 25 minutes

2 pounds assorted baby beets
    with tops
1 tablespoon olive oil
Brown Sugar Vinaigrette
5 cups loosely packed baby
    lettuces

1 cup crumbled Gorgonzola
    cheese
1 cup lightly salted roasted pecan
    halves

1. Preheat oven to 400°. Trim beet tops to ½ inch; gently wash beets. Place beets in a single layer in a shallow baking pan; drizzle with oil, tossing gently to coat. Cover pan tightly with aluminum foil.
2. Bake at 400° for 40 minutes or until tender. Transfer to a wire rack, and let cool 30 minutes.
3. Peel beets, and cut in half. Gently toss beets with ⅓ cup Brown Sugar Vinaigrette. Arrange lettuces on a serving platter. Top with beet mixture, Gorgonzola cheese, and pecans; serve with remaining Brown Sugar Vinaigrette.

Brown Sugar Vinaigrette

Makes ⅔ cup ▪ Prep: 5 minutes ▪ Total: 5 minutes

⅓ cup white balsamic vinegar
1 large shallot, minced
2 tablespoons light brown sugar
½ teaspoon freshly ground
    pepper

½ teaspoon vanilla extract
¼ teaspoon salt
⅓ cup olive oil

1. Whisk together vinegar, shallot, sugar, pepper, vanilla, and salt in a small bowl. Add oil in a slow, steady stream, whisking constantly until smooth.

from **Southern Living**

meal maker

PICK A MAIN DISH

- Italian Pot Roast, page 55

OR

- spiral-cut ham

ADD A DESSERT

- Caramel-Pecan-Pumpkin Bread Puddings, page 233

vegetable sides & salads

QUICK TIP

Keep beets from bleeding onto your baking pan by trimming the tops but leaving part of the stems in place while they roast.

- Avocado Chicken Salad, page 10

OR

- Grilled Baby Back Ribs with Sticky Brown Sugar Glaze, page 72

OR

- Smoked Salmon Sandwich on Pumpernickel, page 93

ADD A DESSERT

- Brown Sugar-Cinnamon Peach Pie, page 238

great for company

Broccoli Slaw with Candied Pecans

Makes 6 servings ▪ Prep: 25 minutes ▪ Total: 1 hour, 25 minutes

1 pound fresh broccoli
1 cup mayonnaise
½ cup thinly sliced green onions
⅓ cup sugar
⅓ cup red wine vinegar
1 teaspoon salt
1 teaspoon lemon zest
¼ teaspoon ground red pepper
½ small head napa cabbage (about 1 pound), thinly sliced*
½ cup golden raisins
1 (3.5-ounce) package roasted glazed pecan pieces

1. Cut broccoli florets from stems; separate florets into small pieces using a paring knife. Peel away tough outer layer of stems; finely chop stems.
2. Whisk together mayonnaise and next 6 ingredients in a large bowl; add cabbage, raisins, and broccoli, and stir to coat. Cover and chill 1 hour. Stir in pecans just before serving.
Note: 1 (16-ounce) package coleslaw mix may be substituted.

from **Southern Living**

SCAN THIS PHOTO to see and save the shopping list.

meal maker

PICK A MAIN DISH

- Grilled Chicken Florentine Pasta, page 23

OR

- veggie and cheese frozen pizza

ADD A DESSERT

- Key Lime Ice Cream Pie, page 243

healthy choice

Buttery Lemon Broccolini

Makes 4 servings ▪ Prep: 10 minutes ▪ Total: 25 minutes

4 quarts water
1⅛ teaspoons salt, divided
2 (6-ounce) packages Broccolini
1 tablespoon butter, softened

½ teaspoon grated lemon rind
1½ teaspoons fresh lemon juice
⅛ teaspoon black pepper

1. Bring 4 quarts water to a boil in a large saucepan; add 1 teaspoon salt. Cook Broccolini in batches for 5 minutes; remove with a slotted spoon. Drain. Discard water.
2. Combine butter, rind, and juice, stirring with a fork until well blended. Return Broccolini to pan over medium-high heat; stir in butter mixture, remaining ⅛ teaspoon salt, and pepper, tossing gently to coat.

For nutritional information on this recipe, please turn to the appendix on pages 248–251.

from CookingLight

meal maker

PICK A MAIN DISH

- Baked Penne with Turkey, page 39

OR

- Sesame Tuna with Edamame and Soba, page 97

ADD A DESSERT

- Bittersweet Fudge with Sea Salt, page 222

healthy choice

Broccoli Rabe with Garlic and Golden Raisins

Makes 4 servings ■ Prep: 20 minutes ■ Total: 20 minutes

1 pound broccoli rabe (rapini)
1 tablespoon extra-virgin olive oil
⅛ teaspoon crushed red pepper
3 garlic cloves, thinly sliced

¼ cup golden raisins
¼ teaspoon kosher salt
¼ teaspoon freshly ground black pepper

1. Bring 8 cups of water to a boil in a large saucepan. Cut broccoli rabe into 2-inch pieces. Cook broccoli rabe in boiling water 2 minutes; drain.
2. Heat a large nonstick skillet over medium heat. Add olive oil to pan; swirl to coat. Add crushed red pepper and garlic to pan; cook 30 seconds, stirring occasionally. Add broccoli rabe and raisins to pan; cook 2 minutes. Stir in salt and black pepper.

For nutritional information on this recipe, please turn to the appendix on pages 248–251.

from CookingLight

QUICK TIP

Use kitchen shears to quickly cut broccoli rabe, or gather into a large bunch and cut stalks crosswise into 2-inch pieces using a sharp chef's knife.

vegetable sides & salads

meal maker

PICK A MAIN DISH

- Smoke-Roasted Turkey Breast with Pomegranate-Thyme Glaze, page 41

OR

- rotisserie chicken

ADD A DESSERT

- Roasted Banana Bars with Browned Butter–Pecan Frosting, page 219

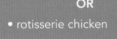

Bacon-Brown Sugar Brussels Sprouts

Makes 6 to 8 servings ▪ Prep: 10 minutes ▪ Total: 25 minutes

4 bacon slices
1 (14-ounce) can chicken broth
1 tablespoon brown sugar

1 teaspoon salt
1½ pounds Brussels sprouts, trimmed and halved

1. Cook bacon in a Dutch oven over medium heat 10 minutes or until crisp. Remove bacon, and drain on paper towels, reserving drippings in Dutch oven. Crumble bacon.

2. Add broth, brown sugar, and salt to drippings in Dutch oven, and bring to a boil. Stir in Brussels sprouts. Cover and cook 6 to 8 minutes or until tender. Transfer to a serving bowl using a slotted spoon, and sprinkle with bacon. Serve immediately.

from **Southern Living**

healthy choice

Steamed Carrots with Garlic-Ginger Butter

Makes 4 servings ▪ Prep: 10 minutes ▪ Total: 25 minutes

---

2 garlic cloves, minced
1 pound baby carrots with tops,
  peeled
1 tablespoon butter
1 teaspoon minced peeled fresh
  ginger

1 tablespoon chopped fresh
  cilantro
½ teaspoon grated lime rind
1 tablespoon fresh lime juice
¼ teaspoon salt

1. Prepare garlic, and let stand 10 minutes.
2. Steam carrots, covered, 10 minutes or until tender.
3. Heat butter in large nonstick skillet over medium heat. Add garlic and ginger to pan; cook 1 minute, stirring constantly. Remove from heat; stir in carrots, cilantro, and remaining ingredients.

For nutritional information on this recipe, please turn to the appendix on pages 248–251.

from CookingLight

meal maker

PICK A MAIN DISH

• Rosemary-Garlic Chicken
  Quarters, page 29

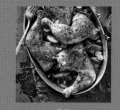

OR

• Roast Leg of Lamb with
  Chile-Garlic Sauce, page 78

OR

• Creamy Spring Pasta,
  page 130

ADD A DESSERT

• White and Dark Chocolate
  Pudding Parfaits, page 237

vegetable sides
& salads

QUICK TIP

Be sure to use true baby carrots with tops. The texture of baby carrots sold in bags will be too tough for this recipe.

PICK A MAIN DISH

- Chili-Lime Drumsticks, page 28

OR

- Cuban Sandwiches, page 62

OR

- Cheesy Corn-and-Black-Bean Quesadillas, page 138

ADD A DESSERT

- Mini Berry Cobblers, page 224

great for company

Creamy Lime Slaw

Makes 8 servings ▪ Prep: 30 minutes ▪ Total: 30 minutes

---

4 green onions
½ head napa cabbage, sliced thinly
½ head red cabbage, sliced thinly
½ cup cilantro leaves

2 limes
½ cup nonfat Greek yogurt
1½ tablespoons sugar
1 teaspoon kosher salt
½ teaspoon pepper

1. Slice green onions long and on the bias so you have pieces similar in shape to the cabbage. Toss together onions, cabbages, and cilantro in a large bowl.
2. Zest both limes and juice 1 lime. In a bowl, mix lime zest and juice, yogurt, sugar, salt, and pepper. Pour dressing over cabbage mixture; stir to combine.

For nutritional information on this recipe, please turn to the appendix on pages 248–251.

from **Sunset**

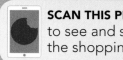
SCAN THIS PHOTO to see and save the shopping list.

SCAN THIS PHOTO
to see and save
the shopping list.

healthy choice

Curried Cauliflower with Capers

Makes 6 servings ▪ Prep: 10 minutes ▪ Total: 40 minutes

---

6 cups cauliflower florets (about 1 large head)
¼ cup extra-virgin olive oil, divided
2 teaspoons grated lemon rind
2 tablespoons lemon juice
½ teaspoon salt
½ teaspoon curry powder
¼ teaspoon freshly ground black pepper
⅓ cup caperberries, thinly sliced
¼ cup chopped fresh flat-leaf parsley
¼ cup capers, drained

1. Preheat oven to 450°.
2. Combine cauliflower and 1 tablespoon oil on a jelly-roll pan, tossing to coat. Bake at 450° for 30 minutes or until browned, turning once.
3. Combine remaining 3 tablespoons oil, lemon rind, and next 4 ingredients (through black pepper) in a large bowl; stir with a whisk. Add roasted cauliflower, caperberries, parsley, and capers to bowl; toss mixture well to combine.

For nutritional information on this recipe, please turn to the appendix on pages 248–251.

from Cooking Light

meal maker

PICK A MAIN DISH

- Quinoa Salad with Chicken, Avocado, and Oranges, page 25

OR

- Indian-Spiced Lentils and Lamb, page 75

OR

- rotisserie chicken and boil-in-bag rice

ADD A DESSERT

- Honeyed Apples with Ice Cream, page 223

vegetable sides & salads

QUICK TIP

Look for olive-size caperberries—the immature fruit of the caper bush—at gourmet grocers or specialty stores.

meal maker

PICK A MAIN DISH

- Skillet Chicken Pot Pie, page 11

OR

- Real Buttermilk Fried Chicken, page 33

OR

- pulled pork from the deli

ADD A DESSERT

- Luscious Lemon Bars, page 217

healthy choice

Balsamic Collard Greens

Makes 5 servings ▪ Prep: 10 minutes ▪ Total: 3 hours, 45 minutes

3 bacon slices
1 cup chopped onion
1 (16-ounce) package chopped
　fresh collard greens
¼ teaspoon salt
2 garlic cloves, minced

1 bay leaf
1 (14.5-ounce) can fat-free,
　lower-sodium chicken broth
3 tablespoons balsamic vinegar
1 tablespoon honey

1. Cook bacon in a large Dutch oven over medium heat until crisp. Remove bacon from pan; crumble. Add onion to drippings in pan; sauté 5 minutes or until tender. Add collard greens, and cook 2 to 3 minutes or until greens begin to wilt, stirring occasionally.

2. Place collard green mixture, salt, and next 3 ingredients (through broth) in a 3-quart electric slow cooker. Cover and cook on LOW for 3½ to 4 hours.

3. Combine balsamic vinegar and honey in a small bowl. Stir vinegar mixture into collard greens just before serving. Sprinkle with bacon.

For nutritional information on this recipe, please turn to the appendix on pages 248–251.

from Oxmoor House.

Grilled Corn Poblano Salad with Chipotle Vinaigrette

Makes 6 to 8 servings ▪ Prep: 10 minutes ▪ Total: 30 minutes

3 ears corn, husks removed	**½ teaspoon kosher salt**
1 poblano chile	**1 avocado, cut into chunks**
3 tablespoons canola oil, divided	**¼ cup cilantro leaves**
1 tablespoon lime juice	**½ cup slivered sweet onion,**
1 teaspoon finely chopped	**rinsed, patted dry**
canned chipotle chile	

1. Heat grill to high (450° to 550°). Rub corn and poblano with 1 tablespoon oil. Grill both, turning occasionally, until poblano is mostly blackened, 5 to 10 minutes, and some corn kernels have browned, 10 to 20 minutes. Let cool.

2. Cut corn kernels from cobs into a large bowl. Peel and seed poblano, cut into ½-inch pieces, and add to corn. In a small bowl, whisk remaining oil with lime juice, chipotle chile, and salt.

3. Stir avocado, cilantro, and onion into corn mixture along with chipotle dressing.

For nutritional information on this recipe, please turn to the appendix on pages 248–251.

from *Sunset*

meal maker

PICK A MAIN DISH

- Chicken Enchiladas, page 12

OR

- Grilled Fish Tacos with Tomato-Green Onion Relish, page 82

OR

- Mexicali Meatless Tostadas, page 142

ADD A DESSERT

- Flourless Peanut Butter-Chocolate Chip Cookies, page 216

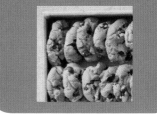

vegetable sides & salads

QUICK TIP

When cutting corn kernels from the cob, stand the cob in a bowl and slice down the sides; the bowl corrals the flying kernels.

meal maker

PICK A MAIN DISH

- Flank Steak Salad with Plums and Blue Cheese, page 53

OR

- frozen chicken fingers

ADD A DESSERT

- Caramel-Pecan-Pumpkin Bread Puddings, page 233

QUICK TIP

For the creamiest corn, use a corn cutter and a creamer instead of a knife to remove the kernels from the cob.

great for company

Creamed Silver Queen Corn

Makes 6 to 8 servings ▪ Prep: 20 minutes ▪ Total: 50 minutes

13 ears fresh corn, husks removed
1 cup milk
1 tablespoon unsalted butter
½ teaspoon salt
⅛ teaspoon freshly ground pepper

1. Remove silks from corn. Use a corn cutter and creamer set over a bowl to cut and cream the kernels from the cobs.

2. Transfer creamed corn to a large skillet. Add milk and next 2 ingredients. Cook over low heat, stirring often, 30 minutes. (If corn becomes too thick, add more milk to desired consistency.) Sprinkle with pepper.

from Southern Living

quick + easy

Caramelized Spicy Green Beans

Makes 4 servings ▪ Prep: 10 minutes ▪ Total: 20 minutes

1 pound fresh haricots verts (tiny green beans)
2 tablespoons light brown sugar
1 tablespoon soy sauce
½ teaspoon dried crushed red pepper

1 medium-size red bell pepper, sliced
½ medium-size sweet onion, sliced
1 teaspoon peanut oil
¾ teaspoon seasoned salt

1. Cook green beans in boiling salted water to cover 1 minute; drain. Plunge beans into ice water to stop the cooking process; drain well, pressing between paper towels.
2. Stir together brown sugar, soy sauce, and dried crushed red pepper.
3. Sauté bell pepper, onion, and green beans in hot peanut oil in a large skillet over high heat 3 to 5 minutes or until beans look blistered. Sprinkle with seasoned salt. Remove from heat; add soy sauce mixture to green bean mixture, and stir to coat.

from **Southern Living**

meal maker

PICK A MAIN DISH

• Greek Chicken Bread Salad, page 20

OR

• Scallops with Capers and Brown Butter Sauce, page 110

OR

• grilled shrimp

ADD A DESSERT

• So Good Brownies, page 220

vegetable sides & salads

SCAN THIS PHOTO to see and save the shopping list.

Roasted Squash and Kale Salad

Makes 4 servings ▪ Prep: 15 minutes ▪ Total: 45 minutes

1 butternut squash
2 tablespoons olive oil
3 tablespoons brown sugar
½ teaspoon salt
½ teaspoon pepper
1 pound kale, thinly sliced
1 cucumber, peeled and julienned
¼ cup thinly sliced red onion
2 teaspoons low-sodium soy sauce
1 tablespoon fresh lime juice
2 teaspoons sesame oil
1 teaspoon sugar
2 tablespoons creamy peanut butter
2 teaspoons minced fresh ginger
1 tablespoon water

1. Preheat oven to 400°. Peel, seed, and cut butternut squash into 1-inch chunks. Toss with olive oil, brown sugar, salt, and pepper; bake at 400° for 25 minutes.

2. Remove from oven; cool. Toss with kale, cucumber, and onion. In a blender, purée soy sauce, lime juice, sesame oil, sugar, peanut butter, ginger, and water. Drizzle salad with dressing; serve.

For nutritional information on this recipe, please turn to the appendix on pages 248–251.

from **Health**

meal maker

PICK A MAIN DISH

• Cassoulet in a Flash, page 42

OR

• Spiced Pork Tenderloin with Sautéed Apples, page 65

ADD A DESSERT

• Chocolate-Caramel Pecan Pie, page 240

QUICK TIP

Knock out your daily dose of vitamin K by dining on one serving of this hearty side dish.

vegetable sides & salads

meal maker

PICK A MAIN DISH

- Country Ham Carbonara, page 70

OR

- Chicken in Wine Sauce, page 30

ADD A DESSERT

- Tart Lemon Ice with Crushed Strawberries, page 244

QUICK TIP

Serve the roasted kale hot from the oven to prevent the leaves from losing their crispy texture as the dish stands.

Garlic-Roasted Kale

Makes 4 servings ▪ Prep: 5 minutes ▪ Total: 25 minutes

3½ teaspoons extra-virgin olive oil
¼ teaspoon kosher salt
1 garlic clove, thinly sliced
10 ounces kale, stems removed and chopped
1 teaspoon sherry vinegar

1. Arrange oven racks in center and lower third of oven. Preheat oven to 425°. Place a large jelly-roll pan in oven for 5 minutes.
2. Combine first 4 ingredients in a large bowl; toss to coat. Place kale mixture on hot pan, spreading with a silicone spatula to separate leaves. Bake at 425° for 7 minutes. Stir kale. Bake an additional 5 minutes or until edges of leaves are crisp and center is tender.
3. Place kale in a large bowl. Drizzle with vinegar; toss to combine. Serve immediately.

For nutritional information on this recipe, please turn to the appendix on pages 248–251.

from CookingLight

meal maker

PICK A MAIN DISH

- Corn-and-Crab Chowder, page 100

OR

- Bean and Sausage Stew, page 36

OR

- grilled chicken sausages

ADD A DESSERT

- Chewy Caramel Apple Cookies, page 214

Waldorf Spinach Salad

Makes 6 servings ▪ Prep: 25 minutes ▪ Total: 25 minutes

¼ cup honey
3 tablespoons vegetable oil
2 tablespoons cider vinegar
½ teaspoon dry mustard
¼ teaspoon ground cinnamon
1 garlic clove, pressed
⅛ teaspoon salt
1 (9-ounce) package fresh
   spinach, torn

2 large Gala apples, thinly sliced
4 ounces extra-sharp white
   Cheddar cheese, shaved
1 cup thinly sliced celery
1 cup honey-roasted cashews
½ cup golden raisins

1. Whisk together first 7 ingredients in a large serving bowl until well blended. Add spinach and remaining ingredients, tossing gently to coat. Serve immediately.

from Southern Living

vegetable sides & salads

SCAN THIS PHOTO to see and save the shopping list.

quick + easy

Summer Squash Ribbons with Lemon and Parmesan

Makes 4 servings ▪ Prep: 10 minutes ▪ Total: 10 minutes

1½ pounds summer squash and zucchini

2 tablespoons extra-virgin olive oil

2 tablespoons fresh lemon juice

2 ounces Parmesan cheese (¾ cup), shaved

½ teaspoon kosher salt

½ teaspoon pepper

1. Cut the squash and zucchini into long, thin strips using a vegetable peeler (discard the seedy cores). Place in a large bowl. Add the oil, lemon juice, Parmesan, salt, and pepper and toss gently to combine. Serve immediately.

For nutritional information on this recipe, please turn to the appendix on pages 248–251.

from **REAL SIMPLE**

meal maker

PICK A MAIN DISH

- Pork and Tomato Skillet Sauté, page 61

OR

- Simple Lobster Risotto, page 104

OR

- grilled chicken

ADD A DESSERT

- Last-Minute Tropical Sherbet, page 245

QUICK TIP

To make summer squash ribbons, simply cut off the ends of the squash, then using a vegetable peeler, peel from top to bottom using long, firm, sweeping motions.

vegetable sides & salads

meal maker

PICK A MAIN DISH

- Turkey Sausage Lasagna, page 34

OR

- frozen Italian sausage pizza

ADD A DESSERT

- Bittersweet Fudge with Sea Salt, page 222

quick + easy

Lemon-Garlic Swiss Chard

Makes 4 servings ▪ Prep: 10 minutes ▪ Total: 10 minutes

1 tablespoon extra-virgin olive oil
1 tablespoon minced garlic
12 cups Swiss chard, chopped
 (about 10 ounces)
2 tablespoons water
1½ teaspoons fresh lemon juice

⅛ teaspoon freshly ground black
 pepper
4 teaspoons shaved fresh
 Parmesan cheese
Lemon wedges

1. Heat a large skillet over medium-high heat. Add oil to pan; swirl to coat. Add garlic; sauté 2 minutes or until garlic begins to brown. Add Swiss chard and 2 tablespoons water to pan; cook 3 minutes or until chard wilts. Stir in lemon juice and pepper. Sprinkle with cheese. Serve with lemon wedges.

For nutritional information on this recipe, please turn to the appendix on pages 248–251.

from Cooking Light

meal maker

PICK A MAIN DISH

• Tilapia Piccata, page 96

OR

• Browned Butter Gnocchi with Broccoli and Nuts, page 133

ADD A DESSERT

• Strawberry-Rhubarb Ice Cream, page 246

vegetable sides & salads

Mozzarella, Tomato, and Basil Salad

Makes 8 servings ▪ Prep: 10 minutes ▪ Total: 10 minutes

6 large ripe tomatoes
1½ pounds fresh mozzarella
½ bunch of fresh basil
Salt and pepper

Olive oil
Balsamic vinegar
Fresh basil leaves

1. Slice tomatoes and mozzarella. Thinly slice basil. On a serving platter, alternate slices of tomato and mozzarella. Sprinkle with basil. Season lightly with salt and pepper. Serve with olive oil and balsamic vinegar on the side. Garnish with basil leaves.

For nutritional information on this recipe, please turn to the appendix on pages 248–251.

from all you

SCAN THIS PHOTO
to see and save
the shopping list.

Everyday Roast Vegetables

Makes 4 servings ▪ Prep: 10 minutes ▪ Total: 1 hour

1 pound carrots, peeled and cut lengthwise
1 pound parsnips, peeled and cut lengthwise
1 pound beets, peeled and cut into wedges
1 red onion, cut into wedges
3 tablespoons extra-virgin olive oil
¼ teaspoon salt
¼ teaspoon black pepper
1 orange, cut in half
½ cup coarsely chopped fresh parsley, for garnish

1. Preheat oven to 400°. In a bowl, toss carrots, parsnips, beets, and onion with olive oil; season with salt and pepper.

2. Spread vegetables in a single layer on roasting pan, leaving as much space as possible between each. Roast at 400° until lightly browned and just tender (50 to 60 minutes), stirring halfway through baking. Remove; squeeze orange juice over top. Toss and transfer to platter. Serve with parsley.

For nutritional information on this recipe, please turn to the appendix on pages 248–251.

from **Health**

meal maker

PICK A MAIN DISH

- Spicy Basil Chicken, page 27

OR

- Fresh Tomato Basil Pizza, page 124

OR

- quartered rotisserie chicken

ADD A DESSERT

- White and Dark Chocolate Pudding Parfaits, page 237

vegetable sides & salads

meal maker

PICK A MAIN DISH

- Caramelized Onion–and–Blue Cheese Mini Burgers, page 46

OR

- Creamy Four-Cheese Macaroni, page 134

ADD A DESSERT

- Peanut Butter Ice Cream Sandwiches, page 247

QUICK TIP

For more tender zucchini, leave slices in the pan an extra 1 minute on each side. When the flesh starts to look translucent, the zucchini is done.

quick + easy

Grilled Zucchini with Sea Salt

Makes 4 servings ▪ Prep: 10 minutes ▪ Total: 10 minutes

2 teaspoons extra-virgin olive oil
¼ teaspoon coarse sea salt
¼ teaspoon freshly ground black pepper

2 medium zucchini, cut diagonally into ½-inch-thick slices

1. Preheat grill pan over medium-high heat. Combine all ingredients in a bowl; toss well to coat. Arrange zucchini in a single layer in pan; grill 4 minutes, turning after 2 minutes.

For nutritional information on this recipe, please turn to the appendix on pages 248–251.

from CookingLight

Lavender-Scented Summer Fruit Salad

Makes 4 servings ▪ Prep: 10 minutes ▪ Total: 1 hour, 25 minutes

2 tablespoons honey or agave
  nectar
¾ teaspoon dried lavender
⅛ teaspoon freshly ground black
  pepper
Pinch salt
1 tablespoon fresh lime juice
1 peach, sliced into ½-inch-thick
  wedges

1 nectarine, sliced into
  ½-inch-thick wedges
1 large plum, sliced into
  ½-inch-thick wedges
1 cup raspberries
1 cup blackberries
¾ cup blueberries
1 tablespoon small whole mint
  leaves

1. Combine honey, ⅓ cup water, lavender, pepper, and salt in a small saucepan. Bring to a simmer over medium heat, stirring until honey has dissolved. Remove from heat, and cover; let steep 10 to 15 minutes or until room temperature. Strain into a serving bowl; discard lavender and stir in lime juice.

2. Add peach, nectarine, and plum wedges to honey mixture, and toss well. Add berries and mint, and toss gently to combine. Refrigerate 1 hour or until chilled. Serve.

For nutritional information on this recipe, please turn to the appendix on pages 248–251.

from **Health**

meal maker

PICK A MAIN DISH

- Grilled Chicken Sliders and Apricot Chutney Spread, page 26

OR

- Chickpeas in Curried Coconut Broth, page 137

ADD A DESSERT

- So Good Brownies, page 220

QUICK TIP

Find dried lavender in the spice section of the supermarket or substitute ¼ cup coarsely chopped mint leaves in place of the lavender.

vegetable sides & salads

meal maker

PICK A MAIN DISH

- White Lightning Chicken Chili, page 14

OR

- Gingery Butternut Squash and Tofu Curry, page 143

OR

- pulled pork from the deli on bakery buns

ADD A DESSERT

- Red Velvet Cupcakes, page 230

great for company

New-Fashioned Apple and Raisin Slaw

Makes 8 servings ▪ Prep: 10 minutes ▪ Total: 10 minutes

½ cup light sour cream
3 tablespoons reduced-fat mayonnaise
1½ tablespoons white balsamic vinegar
1 teaspoon sugar
½ teaspoon black pepper
¼ teaspoon salt
2 cups unpeeled chopped Rome apple (about 1 medium)
1 cup golden raisins
1 (16-ounce) package cabbage-and-carrot coleslaw

1. Combine the first 6 ingredients in a large bowl, stirring with a whisk. Add chopped apple, raisins, and coleslaw; toss to combine.

For nutritional information on this recipe, please turn to the appendix on pages 248–251.

from Cooking Light

great for company

Melon Ball Salad with Lime Syrup

Makes 8 servings ▪ Prep: 20 minutes ▪ Total: 3 hours, 5 minutes

¾ cup sugar
½ cup fresh lime juice
2 tablespoons finely grated lime
 zest
1 cantaloupe (about 3 pounds)

1 honeydew (about 4½ pounds)
½ baby seedless watermelon
 (about 2½ pounds)
Fresh mint sprigs

1. Combine sugar, lime juice, and ¼ cup water in a small saucepan. Stir over medium-high heat until sugar has dissolved, about 5 minutes. Remove from heat and add lime zest. Cover pan and set aside for 15 minutes. Strain into a small bowl, cover and refrigerate until thoroughly chilled, at least 2 hours. (Can be made up to 3 days in advance.)
2. Cut each melon in half, remove and discard seeds, and scoop flesh with a sharp 1-inch melon baller. Place all melon balls in a large bowl, cover, and refrigerate until 30 minutes before serving.
3. Pour lime syrup over melon balls. Cover and chill for at least 30 minutes before serving. Divide into 8 tumblers and garnish with mint, if desired.

For nutritional information on this recipe, please turn to the appendix on pages 248–251.

from all you

meal maker

PICK A MAIN DISH

• Pasta Pork Bolognese, page 58

OR

• Tuna Niçoise Salad with Roasted Green Beans and Potatoes, page 99

ADD A DESSERT

• Flourless Peanut Butter-Chocolate Chip Cookies, page 216

QUICK TIP

Make the lime syrup up to three days ahead and chill until ready to serve.

vegetable sides & salads

BULGUR WHEAT SALAD WITH
TOMATO AND EGGPLANT,
page 193

SCAN THIS PHOTO
to see and save
the shopping list.

bean, grain & potato sides

These simple and versatile supporting players
help your main dish shine.

meal maker

PICK A MAIN DISH

- Pork Tenderloin Salad and Grilled Nectarines, page 64

OR

- Eggplant Parmesan Pizza, page 119

OR

- frozen cheese pizza

ADD A DESSERT

- Tart Lemon Ice with Crushed Strawberries, page 244

quick + easy

Three-Bean Salad

Makes 6 servings ▪ Prep: 20 minutes ▪ Total: 20 minutes

1 (15-ounce) can cannellini beans, drained and rinsed

1 (15-ounce) can chickpeas, drained and rinsed

1 (15-ounce) can kidney beans, drained and rinsed

2 celery stalks, finely chopped

½ red onion, finely chopped

1 cup fresh flat-leaf parsley leaves, finely chopped

2 tablespoons finely chopped fresh rosemary

3 tablespoons fresh lemon juice

¼ cup extra-virgin olive oil

1 teaspoon kosher salt

¼ teaspoon black pepper

1. In a large bowl, combine the cannellini beans, chickpeas, kidney beans, celery, onion, parsley, and rosemary. In a small bowl, whisk together the lemon juice, oil, salt, and pepper. Drizzle the vinaigrette over the salad and toss. Serve at room temperature.

from **REALSIMPLE**

SCAN THIS PHOTO to see and save the shopping list.

SCAN THIS PHOTO to see and save the shopping list.

great for company

Creamy Cannellini Beans with Garlic and Oregano

Makes 8 servings ▪ Prep: 15 minutes ▪ Total: 11 hours

---

2 cups dried cannellini beans
1 gallon water
1¼ teaspoons kosher salt
¼ cup olive oil
¼ teaspoon dried oregano

2 garlic cloves, crushed
1 bay leaf
Freshly ground black pepper
(optional)

1. Sort and wash beans; place in a 6-quart Dutch oven. Cover with water to 2 inches above beans; cover and let stand 8 hours.

2. Drain beans; return to pan. Add 1 gallon water. Bring to a boil; reduce heat, and simmer, uncovered, 2 hours or until tender. Drain beans, reserving ¾ cup cooking liquid. Place beans in a bowl; stir in reserved cooking liquid and salt. Let stand 30 minutes. Wash and dry pan.

3. Heat pan over medium heat. Add oil; swirl to coat. Add oregano, garlic, and bay leaf; sauté 2 minutes or until garlic is golden. Stir in bean mixture. Bring to a simmer; cook 4 minutes or until creamy, stirring frequently. Remove from heat; remove and discard garlic and bay leaf. Sprinkle with pepper, if desired.

For nutritional information on this recipe, please turn to the appendix on pages 248–251.

from Oxmoor House.

meal maker

PICK A MAIN DISH

- Grilled Stuffed Portobello Mushrooms, page 121

OR

- rotisserie chicken

ADD A DESSERT

- Free-form Strawberry Cheesecake, page 229

bean, grain & potato sides

meal maker

PICK A MAIN DISH

- Tofu Steaks with Shiitakes and Veggies, page 147

OR

- grilled or steamed shrimp and cooked rice

ADD A DESSERT

- Cherry-Almond Crisp, page 227

QUICK TIP

Store sesame oil in the refrigerator instead of the pantry to keep it fresher longer.

healthy choice

Edamame Salad

Makes 8 servings ▪ Prep: 20 minutes ▪ Total: 20 minutes

2 tablespoons sesame oil
1 tablespoon rice vinegar
2 teaspoons soy sauce
½ teaspoon Asian chili garlic sauce

1 pound shelled edamame, cooked and cooled
2 green onions, thinly sliced
¼ cup chopped fresh mint
¼ cup sliced almonds

1. In a small bowl, whisk together sesame oil, rice vinegar, soy sauce, and chili sauce. Set aside. In a large bowl, combine edamame, green onions, mint, and almonds. Toss with dressing to coat.

For nutritional information on this recipe, please turn to the appendix on pages 248–251.

from **Sunset**

meal maker

PICK A MAIN DISH

- Greek Lamb Chops and Mint Yogurt Sauce, page 77

OR

- Spinach Pie with Goat Cheese, Raisins, and Pine Nuts, page 122

ADD A DESSERT

- Last-Minute Tropical Sherbet, page 245

quick + easy

Bulgur Wheat Salad with Tomato and Eggplant

Makes 4 servings ▪ Prep: 10 minutes ▪ Total: 20 minutes

1 cup bulgur wheat
1 eggplant, thinly sliced
5 tablespoons extra-virgin olive oil, divided
1 pound cherry tomatoes, cut in half

1 tablespoon red wine vinegar
½ teaspoon kosher salt
¼ teaspoon pepper
1 cup basil leaves, torn

1. Heat broiler.

2. Cook the bulgur according to the package directions.

3. Arrange the eggplant slices on 2 baking sheets. Brush both sides with a total of 3 tablespoons of the oil. Broil the eggplant, 1 baking sheet at a time, until brown, 2 to 3 minutes per side.

4. Transfer to a large bowl. Stir in the tomatoes, vinegar, the remaining 2 tablespoons of oil, salt, and pepper. Fold in the basil.

5. Transfer the bulgur to a large bowl and top with the eggplant and tomato mixture before serving.

For nutritional information on this recipe, please turn to the appendix on pages 248–251.

from **REAL SIMPLE**

bean, grain & potato sides

meal maker

PICK A MAIN DISH

- Pork with Apples, Bacon, and Sauerkraut, page 66

OR

- rotisserie chicken

ADD A DESSERT

- White and Dark Chocolate Pudding Parfaits, page 237

great for company

Sausage and Sourdough Bread Stuffing

Makes 14 servings ▪ Prep: 25 minutes ▪ Total: 2 hours

10 cups (½-inch) cubed sour-dough bread (about 1 pound)
3 tablespoons unsalted butter
2 cups finely chopped onion
1 cup finely chopped celery
15 ounces hot turkey Italian sausage, casings removed
3 tablespoons chopped fresh thyme
3 tablespoons chopped fresh sage

3 tablespoons chopped fresh flat-leaf parsley
½ teaspoon black pepper
2 cups fat-free, lower-sodium chicken broth
1 cup water
1 large egg, lightly beaten
Cooking spray

1. Preheat oven to 350°.
2. Arrange bread in single layers on 2 jelly-roll pans. Bake at 350° for 20 minutes or until golden, rotating pans after 10 minutes. Turn oven off; leave pans in oven for 30 minutes or until bread is crisp.
3. Melt butter in a large skillet over medium heat. Add onion and celery; cook 11 minutes or until tender, stirring occasionally. Transfer vegetables to a large bowl. Add sausage to pan. Increase heat; sauté 8 minutes or until browned, stirring to crumble. Remove sausage from pan using a slotted spoon; add sausage to vegetable mixture. Stir in bread, herbs, and pepper; toss. Combine broth, 1 cup water, and egg, stirring well. Drizzle broth mixture over bread mixture; toss. Spoon mixture into a 13 x 9-inch glass or ceramic baking dish coated with cooking spray; cover with foil. Bake at 350° for 25 minutes. Uncover and cook 20 minutes or until browned.

For nutritional information on this recipe, please turn to the appendix on pages 248–251.

from CookingLight

bean, grain & potato sides

meal maker

PICK A MAIN DISH

- Chicken Kebabs and Nectarine Salsa, page 19

OR

- Mussels with Red Pepper and Chorizo, page 107

ADD A DESSERT

- Roasted Banana Bars with Browned Butter–Pecan Frosting, page 219

quick + easy

Herbed Couscous Pilaf

Makes 4 servings ▪ Prep: 5 minutes ▪ Total: 15 minutes

1 tablespoon olive oil
¼ cup finely chopped shallots
1 cup uncooked couscous
1 cup plus 2 tablespoons fat-free, lower-sodium chicken broth

⅛ teaspoon salt
1 tablespoon chopped fresh flat-leaf parsley
1 teaspoon chopped fresh thyme

1. Heat a small saucepan over medium-high heat. Add oil to pan, swirling to coat. Add shallots; sauté 2 minutes or until tender. Stir in couscous; sauté 1 minute. Add broth and salt; bring to a boil. Cover, remove from heat, and let stand 5 minutes. Fluff with a fork. Stir in parsley and thyme.

For nutritional information on this recipe, please turn to the appendix on pages 248–251.

from Cooking Light

meal maker

PICK A MAIN DISH

- Cheesy Meat Loaf Minis, page 47

OR

- deli fried chicken

ADD A DESSERT

- Real Banana Pudding, page 235

Creamy Grits Casserole

Makes 8 servings ▪ Prep: 10 minutes ▪ Total: 1 hour, 5 minutes

1¼ cups uncooked regular grits
2 cups chicken broth
2 cups milk
1 teaspoon salt
¼ teaspoon ground red pepper
½ cup butter, cut into cubes

1 (10-ounce) block sharp Cheddar cheese, shredded
1 (4-ounce) smoked Gouda cheese round, shredded
2 large eggs, lightly beaten

1. Preheat oven to 350°. Bring grits, chicken broth, and next 3 ingredients to a boil in a medium saucepan over medium-high heat; reduce heat to low, and simmer, stirring occasionally, 4 to 5 minutes or until thickened. Stir in butter and cheeses until melted.

2. Gradually stir about one-fourth of hot grits mixture into eggs; add egg mixture to remaining hot grits mixture, stirring constantly. Pour grits mixture into a lightly greased 2½-quart baking dish.

3. Bake at 350° for 35 to 40 minutes or until golden brown and bubbly around edges. Let stand 5 minutes before serving.

from *Southern Living*

bean, grain & potato sides

meal maker

PICK A MAIN DISH

- Pork Roast with Carolina Gravy, page 69

OR

- Grilled Veggie and Hummus Wraps, page 118

ADD A DESSERT

- Luscious Lemon Bars, page 217

QUICK TIP

Penne or farfalle (bowtie) pasta may be substituted for the orecchiette.

great for company

Marinated Greek-Style Pasta

Makes 14 to 16 servings ▪ Prep: 30 minutes ▪ Total: 2 hours, 30 minutes

1 (16-ounce) package orecchiette
½ pound hard salami slices, cut into strips
¼ pound assorted deli olives, pitted, drained, and cut in half
1 (7-ounce) jar roasted red bell peppers, drained and chopped
6 pepperoncini salad peppers, cut in half lengthwise
½ English cucumber, thinly sliced into half moons
1½ cups bottled Greek vinaigrette with feta, divided
1 pint grape tomatoes, cut in half
¼ cup firmly packed fresh flat-leaf parsley leaves
4 ounces feta cheese, crumbled

1. Cook pasta according to package directions; drain. Rinse with cold running water.
2. Toss together pasta, salami, and next 4 ingredients. Add 1 cup vinaigrette, and toss to coat. Cover and chill 2 to 24 hours.
3. Toss in tomatoes, parsley, and remaining ½ cup vinaigrette just before serving. Sprinkle with feta cheese.

from **Southern Living**

SCAN THIS PHOTO to see and save the shopping list.

SCAN THIS PHOTO to see and save the shopping list.

Quinoa with Roasted Garlic, Tomatoes, and Spinach

Makes 4 servings ▪ Prep: 15 minutes ▪ Total: 1 hour, 15 minutes

1 whole garlic head
1 tablespoon olive oil
1 tablespoon finely chopped
   shallots
¼ teaspoon crushed red pepper
½ cup uncooked quinoa, rinsed
   and drained
1 tablespoon dry white wine

1 cup fat-free, less-sodium
   chicken broth
½ cup baby spinach leaves
⅓ cup chopped seeded tomato
   (1 small)
1 tablespoon shaved fresh
   Parmesan cheese
¼ teaspoon salt

1. Preheat oven to 350°.

2. Remove papery skin from garlic head. Cut garlic head in half crosswise, breaking apart to separate whole cloves. Wrap half of head in foil; reserve remaining garlic for another use. Bake at 350° for 1 hour; cool 10 minutes. Separate cloves; squeeze to extract garlic pulp. Discard skins.

3. Heat oil in a saucepan over medium heat. Add shallots and red pepper to pan; cook 1 minute. Add quinoa to pan; cook 2 minutes, stirring constantly. Add wine; cook until liquid is absorbed, stirring constantly. Add broth; bring to a boil. Cover, reduce heat, and simmer 15 minutes or until liquid is absorbed. Remove from heat; stir in garlic pulp, spinach, tomato, cheese, and salt. Serve immediately.

For nutritional information on this recipe, please turn to the appendix on pages 248–251.

from Cooking Light

meal maker

PICK A MAIN DISH

• Beef Tenderloin Steaks and Balsamic Green Beans, page 49

OR

• Halibut with Smoky Orange Vinaigrette, page 92

OR

• Zucchini and Caramelized Onion Quiche, page 150

ADD A DESSERT

• Strawberry-Rhubarb Ice Cream, page 246

bean, grain & potato sides

SCAN THIS PHOTO to see and save the shopping list.

Brown Rice Pilaf with Almonds and Parsley

Makes 4 servings ▪ Prep: 10 minutes ▪ Total: 35 minutes

2 teaspoons olive oil
1 yellow onion, chopped
1 cup brown rice
2½ cups low-sodium chicken
   broth
1 cup fresh flat-leaf parsley,
   chopped

¼ cup (1 ounce) sliced unsalted
   roasted almonds
½ teaspoon kosher salt
¼ teaspoon pepper

1. Heat the oil in a medium saucepan over medium-high heat. Add the onion and cook, stirring occasionally, until soft, about 6 minutes. Stir in the rice and cook for 1 minute. Add the broth and bring to a boil. Reduce heat and simmer, covered, until the rice is tender and the broth is absorbed, 20 to 25 minutes. Stir in the parsley, almonds, salt, and pepper and transfer to a serving bowl.

For nutritional information on this recipe, please turn to the appendix on pages 248–251.

from **REALSIMPLE**

meal maker

PICK A MAIN DISH

- Maple-Mustard Glazed Chicken, page 22

OR

- Arctic Char and Vegetables in Parchment Hearts, page 86

OR

- Veggie and Tofu Stir-Fry, page 145

ADD A DESSERT

- Honeyed Apples with Ice Cream, page 223

bean, grain & potato sides

meal maker

PICK A MAIN DISH

- Chip-Crusted Fish Fillets, page 88

OR

- Lentil-Barley Burgers with Fiery Fruit Salsa, page 127

ADD A DESSERT

- Peanut Butter Ice Cream Sandwiches, page 247

Home Fries

Makes 6 servings ▪ Prep: 1 hour ▪ Total: 1 hour, 10 minutes

2 pounds Yukon gold or red potato, cubed
2½ tablespoons canola oil, divided
3 cups chopped yellow onion
6 garlic cloves, minced
2 tablespoons butter
½ teaspoon kosher salt
½ teaspoon freshly ground black pepper
¼ cup coarsely chopped fresh flat-leaf parsley

1. Place the potatoes in a microwave-safe dish, and cover with plastic wrap. Microwave at HIGH for 5 minutes. Uncover and cool slightly.
2. Heat a large skillet over medium heat. Add 1½ tablespoons oil to pan; swirl to coat. Add onion; cook 20 minutes or until golden and tender, stirring occasionally. Add garlic; cook 1 minute, stirring constantly. Remove onion mixture from pan. Wipe the pan clean with paper towels.
3. Increase heat to medium-high. Add the remaining 1 tablespoon oil and butter to pan; swirl to coat. Add potato; cook for 4 minutes, without stirring. Turn potatoes over. Cook 6 minutes or until browned, without stirring. Reduce heat to medium-low; cook 10 minutes or until tender and golden brown, stirring occasionally. Remove from heat. Stir in onion mixture, salt, and black pepper; toss. Sprinkle with parsley.

For nutritional information on this recipe, please turn to the appendix on pages 248–251.

from Cooking Light

QUICK TIP

Briefly microwaving the potatoes before frying in the skillet jump-starts the cooking process so they'll be fluffy in the center and crispy on the outside.

SCAN THIS PHOTO
to see and save
the shopping list.

bean, grain &
potato sides

SCAN THIS PHOTO
to see and save
the shopping list.

great for company

Loaded Twice-Baked Potatoes

Makes 8 servings ▪ Prep: 15 minutes ▪ Total: 8 hours, 40 minutes

4 small baking potatoes (about 6 ounces each)
Cooking spray
⅛ teaspoon kosher salt
¼ cup fat-free milk
¼ cup plain fat-free Greek yogurt
2 ounces shredded reduced-fat sharp Cheddar cheese (about ½ cup), divided

¼ teaspoon kosher salt
¼ teaspoon freshly ground black pepper
1 tablespoon chopped fresh chives
2 bacon slices, cooked and crumbled

1. Scrub potatoes; rinse and pat dry with paper towels. Coat potatoes with cooking spray; pierce potatoes with a fork. Rub ⅛ teaspoon kosher salt evenly over potatoes; place in an oval 6-quart electric slow cooker. Cover and cook on LOW for 8 hours or until potatoes are tender. Cool slightly.

2. Cut each potato in half lengthwise; scoop out pulp into a medium microwave-safe bowl, leaving a ⅛-inch-thick shell. Mash pulp with a potato masher. Stir in milk, yogurt, ¼ cup cheese, ¼ teaspoon kosher salt, and pepper. Microwave at HIGH 1 minute or until thoroughly heated.

3. Spoon potato mixture evenly into shells; sprinkle evenly with remaining ¼ cup cheese. Arrange potato halves in bottom of slow cooker. Cover and cook on HIGH for 25 minutes or until thoroughly heated and cheese melts. Sprinkle each potato half with about ½ teaspoon chives and about 1 teaspoon bacon.

For nutritional information on this recipe, please turn to the appendix on pages 248–251.

from Oxmoor House.

meal maker

PICK A MAIN DISH

• Pan-Grilled Flank Steak with Soy-Mustard Sauce, page 52

OR

• grilled pork chops

ADD A DESSERT

• Flourless Peanut Butter-Chocolate Chip Cookies, page 216

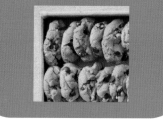

QUICK TIP

Plain fat-free Greek yogurt stands in for sour cream to help lower the calories and fat in this side dish. Layer leftover yogurt with sliced fruit and granola for a healthy snack.

bean, grain & potato sides

- Turkey Tenders, page 37

OR

- Open-Faced Blackened Catfish Sandwiches, page 85

OR

- pulled pork from the deli, bakery buns, and prepared coleslaw

ADD A DESSERT

- Red Velvet Cupcakes, page 230

quick + easy

Oven Roasted Sweet Potato Chips with Ranch Dip

Makes 3 servings ■ Prep: 10 minutes ■ Total: 30 minutes

¾ **pound sweet potatoes (2 medium)**
1 **tablespoon olive oil**
1½ **teaspoons chili powder**

½ **teaspoon salt**
¼ **teaspoon ground cumin**
Store-bought light ranch dressing

1. Preheat oven to 425°.

2. Cut sweet potatoes into ¼-inch-thick slices; set aside. Combine oil, chili powder, salt, and cumin. Add sweet potatoes; toss gently to coat. Cover a lightly oiled nonstick baking sheet with a single layer of potatoes; roast at 425°, turning once, until golden and tender (about 20 minutes). Serve with store-bought light ranch dressing.

For nutritional information on this recipe, please turn to the appendix on pages 248–251.

from Health

meal maker

PICK A MAIN DISH

• Lemon Chicken, page 17

OR

• rotisserie chicken

ADD A DESSERT

• Chocolate-Caramel Pecan Pie, page 240

quick + easy

Rosemary Mashed Sweet Potatoes with Shallots

Makes 4 servings ▪ Prep: 10 minutes ▪ Total: 40 minutes

5½ teaspoons extra-virgin olive oil, divided
½ cup thinly sliced shallots (about 2 medium)
1½ teaspoons brown sugar
1⅓ pounds sweet potatoes, peeled and diced

2 teaspoons finely chopped fresh rosemary
¼ teaspoon coarse sea salt
¼ teaspoon black pepper

1. Heat 4 teaspoons oil in a medium skillet over low heat. Add shallots to pan, and cook for 5 minutes, stirring occasionally. Sprinkle with sugar; cook 20 minutes or until shallots are golden, stirring occasionally.
2. Place potatoes in a medium saucepan; cover with water. Bring to a boil; cook 8 minutes or until tender. Drain. Place potatoes in a large bowl; beat with a mixer at medium speed until smooth. Add rosemary, salt, and pepper; beat until blended. Spoon into a bowl; top with shallots, and drizzle with remaining 1½ teaspoons oil.

For nutritional information on this recipe, please turn to the appendix on pages 248–251.

from CookingLight

bean, grain & potato sides

SCAN THIS PHOTO to see and save the shopping list.

great for company

Roasted Sweet Potatoes and Apples

Makes 10 servings ▪ Prep: 30 minutes ▪ Total: 1 hour, 10 minutes

---

3 pounds orange-flesh sweet potatoes, peeled and cut into 1-inch chunks

3 tablespoons extra-virgin olive oil

2 Fuji apples, peeled and cut into 1-inch chunks

2 Golden Delicious apples, peeled and cut into 1-inch chunks

2 Granny Smith apples, peeled and cut into 1-inch chunks

¼ cup maple syrup

Finely shredded zest of 1 lemon

1 tablespoon fresh lemon juice

1 tablespoon chopped fresh thyme, plus sprigs

About 1½ teaspoons kosher salt

½ teaspoon freshly ground black pepper

Fresh thyme sprigs

1. Preheat oven to 425°. In a large bowl, toss sweet potatoes, oil, apples, syrup, lemon zest and juice, chopped thyme, 1½ teaspoons kosher salt, and pepper until coated.

2. Spread mixture in a single layer in 2 large, oiled, rimmed baking pans. Roast at 425° until sweet potatoes are browned and tender when pierced, 40 minutes, turning chunks every 15 minutes. Transfer to a platter, add more salt to taste, and garnish with thyme sprigs.

For nutritional information on this recipe, please turn to the appendix on pages 248–251.

from **Sunset**

meal maker

PICK A MAIN DISH

• Thai Beef Salad, page 50

OR

• spiral-cut ham

ADD A DESSERT

• Bittersweet Fudge with Sea Salt, page 222

QUICK TIP

This dish can be made up to one day ahead and stored in the fridge. When ready to serve, drizzle with a little olive oil and reheat in a 425° oven in 2 baking pans until hot, 20 minutes.

bean, grain & potato sides

MINI BERRY COBBLERS,
page 224

SCAN THIS PHOTO to see and save the shopping list.

desserts

From chocolate and cookies to fruit and ice cream,
these treats are sure to please every taste bud.

meal maker

PICK A MAIN DISH

- Smoked Salmon Sandwich on Pumpernickle, page 93

OR

- deli fried chicken

ADD A SIDE DISH

- Waldorf Spinach Salad, page 175

great for company

Chewy Caramel Apple Cookies

Makes 36 cookies ▪ Prep: 20 minutes ▪ Total: 1 hour, 30 minutes

½ cup plus 2 tablespoons unsalted butter, softened
1 cup plus 2 tablespoons packed brown sugar
1 large egg
2 tablespoons milk
¾ teaspoon vanilla extract
6.75 ounces gluten-free flour (about 1½ cups)
¾ teaspoon baking soda
¼ teaspoon salt
1½ cups old-fashioned rolled oats
2 chopped peeled apples
Parchment paper
20 caramel candies
2 tablespoons water

1. Preheat oven to 325°.
2. Beat butter and brown sugar with a mixer at medium speed until creamy. Add egg, milk, and vanilla; beat 2 minutes or until light and fluffy.
3. Weigh or lightly spoon flour into dry measuring cups; level with a knife. Combine flour, baking soda, and salt in a bowl, stirring with a whisk. Stir in oats. Add oat mixture to butter mixture, beating at low speed until blended. Stir in apples.
4. Drop dough by 1½ tablespoonfuls 2 inches apart onto baking sheets lined with parchment paper.
5. Bake at 325° for 14 minutes or until golden. Transfer cookies to wire racks; cool completely.
6. Place caramels and water in a small saucepan. Cook over low heat 7 minutes, stirring until smooth. Remove from heat. Drizzle warm glaze over cookies. Let stand 15 minutes or until caramel is completely set. Store in an airtight container for up to 5 days.

For nutritional information on this recipe, please turn to the appendix on pages 248–251.

from Oxmoor House.

SCAN THIS PHOTO to see and save the shopping list.

desserts

- Pan-Grilled Flank Steak with Soy-Mustard Sauce, page 52

OR

- rotisserie chicken

ADD A SIDE DISH

- Grilled Corn Poblano Salad with Chipotle Vinaigrette, page 169

OR

- Loaded Twice-Baked Potatoes, page 207

great for company

Flourless Peanut Butter-Chocolate Chip Cookies

Makes 2 dozen ▪ Prep: 10 minutes ▪ Total: 1 hour, 15 minutes

1 cup creamy peanut butter
¾ cup sugar
1 large egg
½ teaspoon baking soda

¼ teaspoon salt
1 cup semisweet chocolate morsels
Parchment paper

1. Preheat oven to 350°. Stir together peanut butter and next 4 ingredients in a medium bowl until well blended. Stir in chocolate morsels.

2. Drop dough by rounded tablespoonfuls 2 inches apart onto parchment paper-lined baking sheets.

3. Bake at 350° for 12 to 14 minutes or until puffed and lightly browned. Cool on baking sheets on a wire rack 5 minutes. Transfer to wire rack, and let cool 15 minutes.

from **Southern Living**

great for company

Luscious Lemon Bars

Makes about 2 dozen ■ Prep: 20 minutes ■ Total: 1 hour, 45 minutes

2¼ cups all-purpose flour, divided	2 cups granulated sugar
½ cup powdered sugar	1 teaspoon lemon zest
1 cup cold butter, cut into pieces	⅓ cup fresh lemon juice
4 large eggs	½ teaspoon baking powder
	Powdered sugar

1. Preheat oven to 350°. Line bottom and sides of a 13 x 9-inch pan with heavy-duty aluminum foil or parchment paper, allowing 2 to 3 inches to extend over sides; lightly grease foil.

2. Stir together 2 cups flour and ½ cup powdered sugar. Cut in butter using a pastry blender or fork until crumbly. Press mixture onto bottom of prepared pan.

3. Bake at 350° for 20 to 25 minutes or until lightly browned.

4. Meanwhile, whisk eggs in a large bowl until smooth; whisk in granulated sugar, lemon zest, and lemon juice. Stir together baking powder and remaining ¼ cup flour; whisk into egg mixture. Pour mixture over hot baked crust.

5. Bake at 350° for 25 minutes or until filling is set. Let cool in pan on a wire rack 30 minutes. Lift from pan, using foil sides as handles. Cool completely on a wire rack (about 30 minutes). Remove foil, and cut into bars; sprinkle with powdered sugar.

from *Southern Living*

meal maker

PICK A MAIN DISH

• Skillet Chicken Pot Pie, page 11

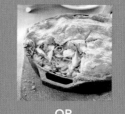

OR

• Tortellini with Peas and Tarragon, page 132

ADD A SIDE DISH

• Simple Sesame Salad, page 156

QUICK TIP

Make the lemon bars ahead, wrap the cooled bars in plastic wrap, place in a zip-top bag, and freeze for up to one month.

desserts

SCAN THIS PHOTO
to see and save
the shopping list.

great for company

Roasted Banana Bars with Browned Butter–Pecan Frosting

Makes 2 dozen ▪ Prep: 30 minutes ▪ Total: 1 hour, 30 minutes

Bars:

2 cups sliced ripe banana (about 3 medium)

⅓ cup packed dark brown sugar

1 tablespoon butter, chilled and cut into small pieces

9 ounces cake flour (about 2¼ cups)

¾ teaspoon baking soda

½ teaspoon baking powder

¼ cup nonfat buttermilk

1 teaspoon vanilla extract

½ cup butter, softened

1¼ cups granulated sugar

2 large eggs

Baking spray with flour

Frosting:

¼ cup butter

2 cups powdered sugar

⅓ cup (3 ounces) ⅓-less-fat cream cheese, softened

1 teaspoon vanilla extract

¼ cup chopped pecans, toasted

1. Preheat oven to 400°.

2. To prepare bars, combine banana, brown sugar, and 1 tablespoon butter in an 8-inch square baking dish. Bake at 400° for 35 minutes, stirring after 17 minutes. Cool slightly.

3. Reduce the oven temperature to 375°.

4. Weigh or lightly spoon cake flour into dry measuring cups; level with a knife. Combine 9 ounces (about 2¼ cups) flour, soda, and baking powder in a medium bowl. Combine banana mixture, buttermilk, and 1 teaspoon vanilla in another medium bowl. Place ½ cup butter and granulated sugar in a large bowl; beat with a mixer at medium speed until well blended. Add eggs to granulated sugar mixture; mix well. Add flour mixture to sugar mixture alternating with banana mixture, beginning and ending with flour mixture.

5. Pour batter into a 13 x 9-inch baking pan coated with baking spray. Bake at 375° for 20 minutes or until a wooden pick inserted in center comes out clean. Cool completely in pan on a wire rack.

6. To prepare frosting, melt ¼ cup butter in a small saucepan over medium heat; cook 4 minutes or until lightly browned. Cool slightly. Combine browned butter, powdered sugar, cream cheese, and 1 teaspoon vanilla in a medium bowl; beat with a mixer until smooth. Spread frosting over cooled bars. Sprinkle with pecans.

For nutritional information on this recipe, please turn to the appendix on pages 248–251.

from Cooking Light

meal maker

PICK A MAIN DISH

• Maple-Mustard Glazed Chicken, page 22

OR

• Scallops with Capers and Brown Butter Sauce, page 110

OR

• Chickpeas in Curried Coconut Broth, page 137

ADD A SIDE DISH

• Bacon-Brown Sugar Brussels Sprouts, page 162

OR

• Herbed Couscous Pilaf, page 196

desserts

meal maker

PICK A MAIN DISH

- Turkey Sausage Lasagna, page 34

OR

- Gingery Butternut Squash and Tofu Curry, page 143

ADD A SIDE DISH

- Caramelized Spicy Green Beans, page 171

OR

- mixed greens and bottled dressing

great for company

So Good Brownies

Makes 16 servings ▪ Prep: 10 minutes ▪ Total: 2 hours

4 (1-ounce) unsweetened chocolate baking squares
¾ cup butter
1½ cups granulated sugar
½ cup firmly packed brown sugar

3 large eggs
1 cup all-purpose flour
1 teaspoon vanilla extract
⅛ teaspoon salt

1. Preheat oven to 350°. Line bottom and sides of an 8-inch square pan with aluminum foil, allowing 2 to 3 inches to extend over sides; lightly grease foil.
2. Microwave chocolate squares and butter in a large microwave-safe bowl at HIGH 1½ to 2 minutes or until melted and smooth, stirring at 30-second intervals. Whisk in granulated and brown sugars. Add eggs, 1 at a time, whisking just until blended after each addition. Whisk in flour, vanilla, and salt.
3. Pour mixture into prepared pan.
4. Bake at 350° for 40 to 44 minutes or until a wooden pick inserted in center comes out with a few moist crumbs. Cool completely on a wire rack (about 1 hour). Lift brownies from pan, using foil sides as handles. Gently remove foil, and cut brownies into 16 squares.

from Southern Living

SCAN THIS PHOTO to see and save the shopping list.

meal maker

PICK A MAIN DISH

- Indian-Spiced Lentils and Lamb, page 75

OR

- Tilapia Piccata, page 96

ADD A SIDE DISH

- Broccoli Rabe with Garlic and Golden Raisins, page 161

OR

- Roasted Sweet Potatoes and Apples, page 211

QUICK TIP

Flaky types of salt like Maldon sea salt flakes show up the best on dark chocolate and won't overpower the sweetness of the fudge. Look for them at spice markets or gourmet grocery stores.

great for company

Bittersweet Fudge with Sea Salt

Makes 36 servings ▪ Prep: 10 minutes ▪ Total: 1 hour, 10 minutes

3 cups mini marshmallows
¼ cup butter
1 (14-ounce) can sweetened condensed milk

12 ounces bittersweet chocolate, chopped
Parchment paper
½ teaspoon flaky sea salt

1. Combine first 3 ingredients in a medium saucepan. Cook over medium heat, stirring constantly, 6 to 7 minutes or until marshmallows are melted. Stir in chocolate.

2. Transfer mixture to an 8-inch square pan lined with parchment paper; sprinkle with salt. Chill about 1 hour or until firm. Cut into squares with a hot knife.

from COASTAL LIVING

quick + easy

Honeyed Apples with Ice Cream

Makes 6 servings ▪ Prep: 10 minutes ▪ Total: 20 minutes

⅓ cup honey
½ teaspoon lemon juice
¼ teaspoon vanilla extract
¼ teaspoon cinnamon

3 tablespoons unsalted butter
3 McIntosh apples, peeled, cored, sliced
1 pint vanilla ice cream

1. Stir honey, lemon juice, vanilla, cinnamon, 2 tablespoons butter, and ¼ cup water in a medium skillet, and bring to a boil over medium-high heat. Stir in apples. Reduce heat to medium and cook, stirring often, until apples are tender and liquid begins to thicken, about 7 minutes. Remove from heat and stir in remaining 1 tablespoon butter. Transfer to a bowl and let cool for 10 minutes.
2. Divide ice cream among 6 bowls. Top with apple mixture and serve immediately.

For nutritional information on this recipe, please turn to the appendix on pages 248–251.

from all you

meal maker

PICK A MAIN DISH

- Stir-Fried Beef with Noodles, page 54

OR

- Chicken-and-Brisket Brunswick Stew, page 13

OR

- Sesame Tuna with Edamame and Soba, page 97

OR

- frozen cheese pizza

ADD A SIDE DISH

- Curried Cauliflower with Capers, page 167

desserts

meal maker

PICK A MAIN DISH

- Pork Roast with Carolina Gravy, page 69

OR

- frozen barbecue chicken pizza

ADD A SIDE DISH

- Creamy Lime Slaw, page 164

QUICK TIP

You can use blackberries, blueberries, raspberries, sliced strawberries or a combination in these cobblers.

Mini Berry Cobblers

Makes 12 servings ▪ Prep: 25 minutes ▪ Total: 1 hour

18 ounces mixed fresh berries (4 cups)
¼ cup sugar
2 tablespoons butter, melted
1 tablespoon cornstarch
1½ cups all-purpose flour
⅓ cup sugar

3 tablespoons minced crystallized ginger
2 teaspoons baking powder
½ teaspoon salt
⅔ cup cold butter, cubed
½ cup buttermilk
Garnish: fresh mint sprigs

1. Preheat oven to 400°. Toss together first 4 ingredients in a medium bowl.

2. Whisk together flour and next 4 ingredients in a large bowl. Cut cold butter into flour mixture with a pastry blender or fork until crumbly. Add buttermilk, stirring just until dry ingredients are moistened. Turn dough out onto a lightly floured surface, and knead 3 to 4 times. Pat into a 6- x 4-inch (1-inch-thick) rectangle. Cut into 6 squares; cut squares diagonally into 12 triangles.

3. Arrange 12 (3½-inch) lightly greased miniature cast-iron skillets on an aluminum foil-lined baking sheet. Divide berry mixture among skillets. Place 1 dough triangle over berry mixture in each skillet.

4. Bake at 400° for 20 to 24 minutes or until fruit bubbles and crust is golden brown. Cool 15 minutes before serving. Serve warm or at room temperature. Garnish with mint sprigs.

from Southern Living

SCAN THIS PHOTO to see and save the shopping list.

desserts

SCAN THIS PHOTO
to see and save
the shopping list.

Cherry-Almond Crisp

Makes 12 servings • Prep: 30 minutes • Total: 1 hour, 35 minutes

1 cup dried tart cherries
1 cup boiling water
2 pounds sweet cherries, pitted
⅔ cup granulated sugar
3 tablespoons all-purpose flour
1 teaspoon vanilla extract
¼ teaspoon ground cinnamon
Cooking spray
3.4 ounces all-purpose flour
  (about ¾ cup)

¾ cup old-fashioned rolled oats
½ cup packed brown sugar
¼ cup sliced almonds
½ teaspoon salt
5 tablespoons unsalted butter,
  melted
¼ teaspoon almond extract
Vanilla ice cream (optional)

1. Combine dried cherries and boiling water in a small bowl; cover and let stand for 30 minutes.
2. Preheat oven to 375°.
3. Combine dried cherries with soaking liquid, 2 pounds sweet cherries, and the next 4 ingredients (through cinnamon) in a large bowl; stir well. Let stand for 15 minutes.
4. Pour the cherry mixture into a 13 x 9-inch glass or ceramic baking dish coated with cooking spray. Bake at 375° for 40 minutes or until thick and bubbly.
5. While cherry mixture bakes, weigh or lightly spoon 3.4 ounces flour into dry measuring cups, and level with a knife. Combine flour, oats, brown sugar, almonds, and salt in a medium bowl, and stir well. Combine butter and almond extract in a small bowl, and drizzle over oat mixture, stirring until moist clumps form.
6. Remove cherry mixture from oven, and sprinkle evenly with the streusel topping. Bake an additional 20 minutes or until streusel is golden brown. Let stand for 5 minutes; serve warm with ice cream, if desired.

For nutritional information on this recipe, please turn to the appendix on pages 248–251.

from CookingLight

meal maker

PICK A MAIN DISH

- Chili-Lime Drumsticks, page 28

OR

- Seared Scallops with Bacon, Cabbage, and Apple, page 108

ADD A SIDE DISH

- Arugula Avocado Salad, page 154

OR

- Edamame Salad, page 192

QUICK TIP

Because fresh tart cherries can be hard to find, we added some dried ones to boost the flavor of this crisp. If you have access to fresh tart cherries, use 3 pounds and omit the dried fruit.

desserts

SCAN THIS PHOTO to see and save the shopping list.

Free-form Strawberry Cheesecake

Makes 6 servings ▪ Prep: 20 minutes ▪ Total: 20 minutes

2 cups fresh strawberries, sliced
¼ cup powdered sugar, divided
1½ cups ready-to-eat cheesecake
   filling
1 teaspoon lime zest

1 tablespoon lime juice
6 crisp gourmet cookies,
   crumbled
Garnishes: crisp gourmet
   cookies, lime slices

1. Stir together strawberries and 2 tablespoons powdered sugar.
2. Stir together cheesecake filling, lime zest, lime juice, and remaining 2 tablespoons powdered sugar.
3. Spoon cheesecake mixture into 6 (6-ounce) glasses or ramekins. Sprinkle with crumbled cookies. Top with strawberries. Garnish, if desired. Serve immediately.
Note: We tested with Philadelphia Ready-To-Eat Cheesecake Filling and Biscoff cookies.

from **Southern Living**

meal maker

PICK A MAIN DISH

- Quinoa Salad with Chicken, Avocado, and Oranges, page 25

OR

- Browned Butter Gnocchi with Broccoli and Nuts, page 133

ADD A SIDE DISH

- Melon Ball Salad with Lime Syrup, page 185

QUICK TIP

Powdered sugar dissolves almost instantly when stirred into berries, while granulated sugar needs standing time. We chose powdered for this quickly assembled recipe.

desserts

meal maker

PICK A MAIN DISH

- Spiced Pork Tenderloin with Sautéed Apples, page 65

OR

- frozen veggie pizza

ADD A SIDE DISH

- New-Fashioned Apple and Raisin Slaw, page 184

OR

- mixed greens and bottled dressing

great for company

Red Velvet Cupcakes

Makes 30 cupcakes ▪ Prep: 30 minutes ▪ Total: 2 hours

Cupcakes:
Cooking spray
10 ounces cake flour (about 2½ cups)
3 tablespoons unsweetened cocoa
1 teaspoon baking soda
1 teaspoon baking powder
1 teaspoon kosher salt
1½ cups granulated sugar
6 tablespoons unsalted butter, softened
2 large eggs

1¼ cups nonfat buttermilk
1½ teaspoons white vinegar
1½ teaspoons vanilla extract
2 tablespoons red food coloring (about 1 ounce)
Frosting:
5 tablespoons butter, softened
4 teaspoons nonfat buttermilk
1 (8-ounce) block cream cheese, softened
3½ cups powdered sugar (about 1 pound)
1¼ teaspoons vanilla extract

1. Preheat oven to 350°.
2. To prepare the cupcakes, place 30 paper muffin cup liners in muffin cups; coat with cooking spray.
3. Weigh or lightly spoon cake flour into dry measuring cups; level with a knife. Combine cake flour, unsweetened cocoa, baking soda, baking powder, and salt in a medium bowl; stir with a whisk. Place granulated sugar and unsalted butter in a large bowl; beat with a mixer at medium speed until well blended (about 3 minutes). Add eggs, 1 at a time, beating well after each addition. Add flour mixture and 1¼ cups nonfat buttermilk alternately to sugar mixture, beginning and ending with flour mixture. Add white vinegar, 1½ teaspoons vanilla, and food coloring; beat well.
4. Spoon batter into prepared muffin cups. Bake at 350° for 20 minutes or until a wooden pick inserted in center comes out clean. Cool in pans 10 minutes on wire racks; remove from pans. Cool completely on wire racks.
5. To prepare frosting, beat 5 tablespoons butter, 4 teaspoons nonfat buttermilk, and cream cheese with a mixer at high speed until fluffy. Gradually add powdered sugar; beat until smooth. Add 1¼ teaspoons vanilla; beat well. Spread frosting evenly over cupcakes.

For nutritional information on this recipe, please turn to the appendix on pages 248–251.

from CookingLight

SCAN THIS PHOTO to see and save the shopping list.

desserts

meal maker

PICK A MAIN DISH

- Grilled Chicken Florentine Pasta, page 23

OR

- Cuban Sandwiches, page 62

ADD A SIDE DISH

- Grilled Asparagus with Caper Vinaigrette, page 155

Grilled Pound Cake with Lemon Cream and Blueberries

Makes 8 servings ▪ Prep: 10 minutes ▪ Total: 10 minutes

½ cup heavy cream
1 tablespoon sugar
¼ cup jarred lemon curd

1 loaf pound cake (about 1 pound), ends trimmed, cut into 8 slices
¾ cup blueberries

1. Preheat grill to medium. Using an electric mixer on high speed, beat cream and sugar until soft peaks form. Fold in lemon curd. Cover and chill.

2. Place cake slices on grate and grill until golden brown on one side, about 2 minutes. Watch carefully, as cake will toast quickly. With a heat-proof spatula, carefully flip slices and grill until golden brown on second side, 1 to 2 minutes longer.

3. To serve, place a slice of grilled pound cake on a plate and top with a generous dollop of lemon cream and some blueberries. Repeat with remaining cake, cream, and berries.

For nutritional information on this recipe, please turn to the appendix on pages 248–251.

from all you

great for company

Caramel-Pecan-Pumpkin Bread Puddings

Makes 11 servings ▪ Prep: 30 minutes ▪ Total: 9 hours, 30 minutes

Bread Puddings:
4 large eggs
2 (15-ounce) cans pumpkin
1½ cups milk
1 cup half-and-half
1 cup granulated sugar
1 teaspoon ground cinnamon
½ teaspoon salt
½ teaspoon ground nutmeg
½ teaspoon vanilla extract

1 (12-ounce) French bread loaf, cut into 1-inch pieces (about 10 cups)

Caramel-Pecan Sauce:
1 cup pecans, chopped
1 cup firmly packed light brown sugar
½ cup butter
1 tablespoon light corn syrup
1 teaspoon vanilla extract

1. Prepare Bread Puddings: Whisk together eggs and next 8 ingredients in a large bowl until well blended. Add bread pieces, stirring to thoroughly coat. Cover with plastic wrap, and chill 8 to 24 hours.

2. Preheat oven to 350°. Spoon bread mixture into 11 lightly greased 6-ounce ramekins. (Ramekins will be completely full, and mixture will mound slightly.) Place on an aluminum foil-lined jelly-roll pan.

3. Bake at 350° for 50 minutes, shielding with foil after 30 minutes.

4. During last 15 minutes of baking, prepare Caramel-Pecan Sauce: Heat pecans in a medium skillet over medium-low heat, stirring often, 3 to 5 minutes or until lightly toasted and fragrant.

5. Cook brown sugar, butter, and corn syrup in a small saucepan over medium heat, stirring occasionally, 3 to 4 minutes or until sugar is dissolved. Remove from heat; stir in vanilla and pecans.

6. Remove bread puddings from oven; drizzle with Caramel-Pecan Sauce. Bake 5 minutes or until sauce is thoroughly heated and begins to bubble.

from Southern Living

meal maker

PICK A MAIN DISH

- Bean and Sausage Stew, page 36

OR

- Beef and Guinness Stew, page 56

OR

- smoked brisket from your favorite BBQ restaurant

ADD A SIDE DISH

- Roasted Baby Beet Salad, page 157

QUICK TIP

If you don't have 11 ramekins in your kitchen, you can make one large bread pudding. Use a 13 x 9-inch baking dish and bake, covered, at 350° for 35 minutes, then uncover and bake for 15 more minutes.

desserts

SCAN THIS PHOTO
to see and save
the shopping list.

Real Banana Pudding

Makes 8 to 10 servings ▪ Prep: 25 minutes ▪ Total: 1 hour, 5 minutes

½ cup sugar
2 tablespoons cornstarch
¼ teaspoon salt
2¼ cups milk
4 large eggs, separated

2 tablespoons unsalted butter
1 teaspoon vanilla extract
3⅓ cups vanilla wafers
4 ripe bananas, sliced
3 tablespoons sugar

1. Preheat oven to 375°. Whisk together first 3 ingredients in a small bowl. Whisk together sugar mixture, milk, and 4 egg yolks in a medium-size heavy saucepan until well blended. Cook over medium heat, stirring constantly, 6 to 8 minutes or until thickened. Remove from heat; stir in butter and vanilla.

2. Layer half of vanilla wafers in an 8-inch square baking dish. Top with half of banana slices and half of pudding. Repeat procedure with remaining wafers, banana slices, and pudding.

3. Beat egg whites at high speed with an electric mixer until foamy. Gradually add 3 tablespoons sugar, beating until sugar dissolves and stiff peaks form. Spread meringue over pudding, sealing to edge of dish.

4. Bake at 375° for 7 to 10 minutes or until golden. Let cool 30 minutes, and serve warm; or chill an additional hour, and serve cold.

from **Southern Living**

meal maker

PICK A MAIN DISH

• Real Buttermilk Fried Chicken, page 33

OR

• Cheesy Meat Loaf Minis, page 47

OR

• Open-Faced Blackened Catfish Sandwiches, page 85

ADD A SIDE DISH

• Balsamic Collard Greens, page 168

OR

• Creamy Grits Casserole, page 197

desserts

SCAN THIS PHOTO
to see and save
the shopping list.

White and Dark Chocolate Pudding Parfaits

Makes 4 servings ▪ Prep: 15 minutes ▪ Total: 2 hours, 15 minutes

⅓ cup plus 2 tablespoons sugar
3 tablespoons cornstarch
2 cups whole milk
1 cup heavy cream
1½ ounces white chocolate, chopped
1½ ounces unsweetened chocolate, chopped
1 teaspoon vanilla extract
1 (12-ounce) bag frozen raspberries, thawed and drained
4 chocolate wafer cookies, crushed

1. Combine ⅓ cup sugar and cornstarch in a medium pot. Whisk in ½ cup milk until smooth. Whisk in remaining milk and cream. Bring to a boil over medium-high heat, stirring. Reduce heat to low; cook, stirring constantly, for 2 minutes.

2. Divide pudding into two bowls. Stir white chocolate into one bowl until melted and smooth. Stir unsweetened chocolate into other bowl until melted and smooth. Stir ½ teaspoon vanilla into each bowl. Press plastic wrap onto surface of both puddings and refrigerate until cold, at least 2 hours and up to 1 day.

3. Combine berries and remaining sugar and let stand, stirring occasionally, until sugar dissolves, about 2 minutes.

4. Divide dark chocolate pudding among 4 (1-cup) glasses. Carefully divide half of white chocolate pudding over dark chocolate pudding layer. Top with raspberries, then remaining half of white chocolate pudding. Sprinkle crushed chocolate wafers on top. Serve immediately, or refrigerate, covered, for up to 2 hours.

For nutritional information on this recipe, please turn to the appendix on pages 248–251.

from all you

meal maker

PICK A MAIN DISH

- Italian Pot Roast, page 55

OR

- Country Ham Carbonara, page 70

OR

- White Lightning Chicken Chili, page 14

ADD A SIDE DISH

- Steamed Carrots with Garlic-Ginger Butter, page 163

desserts

- Rosemary-Garlic Chicken Quarters, page 29

OR

- Crab Cakes with Spicy Rémoulade, page 103

OR

- spiral-cut ham

ADD A SIDE DISH

- Broccoli Slaw with Candied Pecans, page 158

QUICK TIP

Don't make the fresh peach mixture ahead or it will become too juicy and lead to a soggy pie.

great for company

Brown Sugar-Cinnamon Peach Pie

Makes 8 servings ▪ Prep: 30 minutes ▪ Total: 4 hours, 50 minutes

1⅓ cups cold butter
4¼ cups all-purpose flour, divided
1½ teaspoons salt
½ to ¾ cup ice-cold water
8 large fresh, firm, ripe peaches (about 4 pounds)
½ cup firmly packed light brown sugar
⅓ cup granulated sugar
1 teaspoon ground cinnamon
⅛ teaspoon salt
1½ tablespoons butter, cut into pieces
1 large egg, beaten
1½ tablespoons granulated sugar

1. Cut 1⅓ cups butter into small cubes, and chill 15 minutes. Stir together 4 cups flour and 1½ teaspoons salt. Cut butter into flour mixture with a pastry blender until mixture resembles small peas. Gradually stir in ½ cup ice water with a fork, stirring until dry ingredients are moistened and dough begins to form a ball and leaves sides of bowl, adding more ice water, 1 tablespoon at a time, if necessary. Turn dough out onto a piece of plastic wrap; press and shape dough into 2 flat disks. Wrap each disk in plastic wrap, and chill 30 minutes to 24 hours.

2. Preheat oven to 425°. Place 1 dough disk on a lightly floured surface; sprinkle dough lightly with flour. Roll dough to about ¼-inch thickness. Wrap dough around a rolling pin. Place rolling pin over a 9-inch pie plate, and unroll dough over pie plate. Press dough into pie plate. Roll remaining dough disk to about ¼-inch thickness on a lightly floured surface.

3. Peel peaches, and cut into ½-inch-thick slices; cut slices in half. Stir together brown sugar, next 3 ingredients, and remaining ¼ cup flour in a bowl; add peaches, stirring to coat. Immediately spoon peach mixture into piecrust in pie plate, and dot with 1½ tablespoons butter.

4. Carefully place remaining piecrust over filling; press edges of crusts together to seal. Cut off excess crust, and reserve. Crimp edges of pie. Brush top of pie with beaten egg; sprinkle with 1½ tablespoons granulated sugar. Cut 4 to 5 slits in top of pie for steam to escape.

5. Freeze pie 15 minutes. Meanwhile, heat a jelly-roll pan in oven 10 minutes. Place pie on hot jelly-roll pan. Bake at 425° on lower oven rack 15 minutes. Reduce oven temperature to 375°; bake 40 minutes. Cover loosely with aluminum foil to prevent excessive browning, and bake 25 more minutes or until juices are thick and bubbly (juices will bubble through top). Transfer to a wire rack; cool 2 hours before serving.

from Southern Living

SCAN THIS PHOTO to see and save the shopping list.

desserts

meal maker

PICK A MAIN DISH

- Smoke-Roasted Turkey Breast with Pomegranate-Thyme Glaze, page 41

OR

- Creamy Four-Cheese Macaroni, page 134

ADD A SIDE DISH

- Roasted Squash and Kale Salad, page 173

Chocolate-Caramel Pecan Pie

Makes 6 to 8 servings ▪ Prep: 20 minutes ▪ Total: 4 hours, 25 minutes

1½ cups pecan halves and pieces
1 (14.1-ounce) package refrigerated piecrusts
1 cup semisweet chocolate morsels
½ cup whipping cream, divided
1 (8-ounce) package cream cheese, softened
1 cup sugar, divided
1 large egg
28 caramels
¼ cup butter
2 large eggs
1 teaspoon vanilla extract
¼ teaspoon salt

1. Preheat oven to 350°. Bake pecans in a single layer in a shallow pan 8 to 10 minutes or until toasted, stirring halfway through. Cool completely on a wire rack (about 30 minutes). Increase oven temperature to 425°.
2. Unroll piecrusts; stack on a lightly floured surface. Roll stacked piecrusts into a 12-inch circle. Fit piecrust into a 10-inch deep-dish tart pan with removable bottom; press into fluted edges. Trim off excess crust along edges. Line piecrust with aluminum foil or parchment paper, and fill with pie weights or dried beans. Place pan on a foil-lined baking sheet.
3. Bake at 425° for 12 minutes. Remove weights and foil, and bake 4 more minutes. Cool completely on baking sheet on a wire rack (about 15 minutes). Reduce oven temperature to 350°.
4. Microwave chocolate morsels and ¼ cup cream in a microwave-safe bowl at HIGH 1 minute or until melted and smooth, stirring at 30-second intervals.
5. Beat cream cheese and ¼ cup sugar at medium speed with an electric mixer 1 to 2 minutes or until smooth. Add 1 egg, beating at low speed just until blended. Add chocolate mixture, beating just until blended. Spoon batter into prepared crust.
6. Microwave caramels, butter, and remaining ¼ cup cream in a large microwave-safe bowl at HIGH 1 to 2 minutes or until smooth, stirring at 30-second intervals. Whisk together 2 eggs, vanilla, salt, and remaining ¾ cup sugar; whisk into caramel mixture until blended. Stir in pecans; spoon over chocolate mixture in prepared crust.
7. Bake at 350° for 55 minutes to 1 hour and 5 minutes or until center is almost set, shielding edges with aluminum foil after 45 minutes to prevent excessive browning. Cool completely on a wire rack (about 2 hours).

from Southern Living

desserts

SCAN THIS PHOTO to see and save the shopping list.

Key Lime Ice Cream Pie

Makes 8 servings ▪ Prep: 30 minutes ▪ Total: 6 hours, 30 minutes

1⅔ cups sugar, divided
1⅔ cups heavy cream
1 cup whole milk
¼ cup light corn syrup
1 vanilla bean, split in half length-
    wise
1¼ cups graham cracker crumbs
5 tablespoons unsalted butter,
    melted

¼ cup sugar
¼ teaspoon ground cinnamon
Pinch of freshly grated nutmeg
8 large egg yolks
1 teaspoon Key lime zest
1¼ cups fresh Key lime juice
    (about 20 Key limes)
Garnishes: Key lime slices,
    sweetened whipped cream

1. Combine 1 cup sugar and next 3 ingredients in a large saucepan. Scrape seeds from vanilla bean; add seeds and bean to milk mixture. Bring to a boil over high heat. Immediately remove from heat, and let stand 30 minutes. Remove and discard vanilla bean.

2. Preheat oven to 350°. Combine graham cracker crumbs and next 4 ingredients in a medium bowl, tossing until well blended. Press crumbs into a 9-inch glass or ceramic pie plate to form an even crust. Bake at 350° for 8 minutes or until firm to the touch; cool completely, and set aside.

3. Beat egg yolks in a large bowl. Slowly whisk 1 cup warm cream mixture into egg yolks. Add egg mixture to remaining cream mixture, whisking constantly.

4. Cook cream mixture over medium heat, whisking constantly, 5 minutes or until mixture reaches 160° and coats the back of a spoon. Remove from heat; pour through a fine wire-mesh strainer into a bowl. Cool custard completely, stirring occasionally.

5. Combine remaining ⅔ cup sugar and Key lime zest and juice in a bowl, stirring until sugar dissolves. Stir lime juice mixture into cooled custard. Transfer custard to an ice cream maker, and process according to manufacturer's directions.

6. Mound ice cream into prepared crust. Freeze pie 4 hours or overnight. Garnish, if desired.

from COASTAL LIVING

meal maker

PICK A MAIN DISH

- Grilled Baby Back Ribs with Sticky Brown Sugar Glaze, page 72

OR

- Fresh Tomato Basil Pizza, page 124

ADD A SIDE DISH

- Buttery Lemon Broccolini, page 160

QUICK TIP

If you can't find fresh Key limes (the tiny ones), substitute the juice and zest of standard limes or use 1¼ cups bottled Key lime juice.

meal maker

PICK A MAIN DISH

- Chicken Enchiladas,
  page 12

OR

- Mussels with Red Pepper
  and Chorizo, page 107

OR

- Lettuce Wraps with Hoisin-
  Peanut Sauce, page 148

ADD A SIDE DISH

- Garlic-Roasted Kale,
  page 174

OR

- Three-Bean Salad, page 188

healthy choice

Tart Lemon Ice with Crushed Strawberries

Makes 7 servings ▪ Prep: 15 minutes ▪ Total: 7 hours, 45 minutes

1 cup sugar	1 teaspoon sugar
1 cup water	2 tablespoons chopped fresh
1 cup fresh lemon juice	mint
1½ cups quartered strawberries	Lemon zest (optional)

1. Combine 1 cup sugar and 1 cup water in a 2-cup glass measure. Microwave at HIGH 3 to 5 minutes or until sugar dissolves and mixture boils; stir well. Cool completely. Cover and refrigerate simple syrup until thoroughly chilled.

2. Combine lemon juice and simple syrup in a 13 x 9–inch baking dish. Cover and freeze at least 3 hours or until firm. Scrape frozen mixture with the tines of a fork.

3. Place strawberries and 1 teaspoon sugar in a medium bowl. Mash strawberry mixture slightly with a potato masher to release juice. Stir in mint. Cover and let stand at room temperature 30 minutes.

4. Spoon ½ cup lemon mixture into each of 7 bowls; top each serving with about 2 tablespoons strawberry mixture. Garnish with lemon zest, if desired.

For nutritional information on this recipe, please turn to the appendix on pages 248–251.

from Oxmoor House.

healthy choice

Last-Minute Tropical Sherbet

Makes 4 servings ▪ Prep: 15 minutes ▪ Total: 15 minutes

1 (12-ounce) package frozen mango chunks (about 2½ cups)
1 cup frozen pineapple chunks
1 (6-ounce) carton lemon low-fat yogurt
1 teaspoon grated lime rind
Lime slices (optional)

1. Remove mango and pineapple from freezer; let stand at room temperature 10 minutes. Combine mango, pineapple, yogurt, and rind in a food processor; process until smooth. Serve immediately (for soft-serve texture) or freeze in an airtight container for 1 hour 30 minutes (for firmer texture). Garnish with lime slices, if desired.

For nutritional information on this recipe, please turn to the appendix on pages 248–251.

from CookingLight

meal maker

PICK A MAIN DISH

- Chicken Kebabs and Nectarine Salsa, page 19

OR

- Avocado Chicken Salad, page 10

ADD A SIDE DISH

- Summer Squash Ribbons with Lemon and Parmesan, page 177

QUICK TIP

Whirling frozen fruit and yogurt together creates a tangy sherbet with the texture of soft-serve ice cream. You can make it ahead, but don't freeze overnight; the mixture will become icy.

desserts

Strawberry-Rhubarb Ice Cream

Makes 10 servings ▪ Prep: 1 hour ▪ Total: 2 hours, 30 minutes

2½ cups whole milk
¾ cup half-and-half
1 cup sugar, divided
3 large egg yolks
2 cups chopped fresh rhubarb

⅓ cup fruity red wine (such as Merlot)
3 cups chopped fresh strawberries (about 1 pound)

1. Combine milk and half-and-half in a heavy saucepan over medium-high heat. Heat milk mixture to 180° or until tiny bubbles form around edge (do not boil). Combine ½ cup sugar and egg yolks in a large bowl, stirring with a whisk until pale yellow. Gradually add half of hot milk mixture to egg yolk mixture, stirring constantly with a whisk. Pour the egg yolk mixture into pan with remaining milk mixture; cook over medium-low heat until a thermometer registers 160° (about 2 minutes), stirring constantly. Place pan in a large ice-filled bowl for 20 minutes or until custard cools completely, stirring occasionally.

2. Combine remaining ½ cup sugar, rhubarb, and wine in a saucepan over medium-high heat; bring to a boil. Reduce heat, and simmer 8 minutes or until rhubarb is tender and liquid is syrupy. Remove from heat; let stand 10 minutes. Combine rhubarb mixture and strawberries in a blender; process until smooth. Strain mixture through a sieve over a bowl, pressing with a wooden spoon; discard solids. Stir rhubarb mixture into custard mixture.

3. Pour custard into the freezer can of an ice-cream freezer; freeze according to manufacturer's instructions. Drain ice water from freezer bucket; repack with salt and ice. Cover with kitchen towels, and let stand 1 hour or until firm.

For nutritional information on this recipe, please turn to the appendix on pages 248–251.

from CookingLight

great for company

Peanut Butter Ice Cream Sandwiches

Makes 12 servings • Prep: 30 minutes • Total: 1 hour, 30 minutes

1½ cups all-purpose flour
½ teaspoon baking soda
Pinch of salt
½ cup (1 stick) unsalted butter,
   at room temperature
1 cup sugar

1 large egg
1 cup smooth peanut butter
1 teaspoon vanilla extract
3 cups chocolate or strawberry
   ice cream, or a combination,
   softened

1. Preheat oven to 375°. Line 2 large baking sheets with parchment paper.
2. Sift flour, baking soda, and salt together. Using an electric mixer
on medium speed, beat butter and sugar together until light, about 2
minutes. Add egg; mix well. Beat in peanut butter and vanilla. Beat flour
mixture into butter mixture.
3. Roll dough into 1½-inch balls; place 2 inches apart on sheets. Flatten
with a fork in a crisscross design. Bake at 375° until golden, 12 to 15 minutes. Let cool on sheets for 5 minutes; transfer to a rack to cool.
4. Place 1 scoop of ice cream on a cookie, top with another cookie,
and carefully press down. Wrap in plastic wrap and freeze. Repeat with
remaining cookies and ice cream. Freeze for 45 minutes; serve.

For nutritional information on this recipe, please turn to the appendix on pages 248–251.

from all*you*

meal maker

PICK A MAIN DISH

• Turkey Tenders, page 37

OR

• Cheesy Corn-and-Black-
Bean Quesadillas,
page 138

OR

• Grilled Stuffed Portobello
Mushrooms, page 121

ADD A SIDE DISH

• Grilled Zucchini with Sea
Salt, page 182

OR

• mixed baby greens with
bottled dressing

desserts

NUTRITIONAL INFORMATION

poultry

AVOCADO CHICKEN SALAD Amount per serving (1 cup salad and about ½ cup chips): Calories: 345; Fat: 21.1g; Saturated fat: 3.1g; Monounsaturated fat: 12.1g; Polyunsaturated fat: 4.5g; Protein: 19.2g; Carbohydrate: 20.4g; Fiber: 4.5g; Cholesterol: 50mg; Iron: 1.1mg; Sodium: 579mg; Calcium: 52mg

COCONUT-CURRY CHICKEN SOUP Amount per serving (2 cups soup and 1 lime wedge): Calories: 315; Calories from fat: 22%; Fat: 7.8g; Saturated fat: 3.7g; Mono-unsaturated fat: 2.2g; Polyunsaturated fat: 1.3g; Protein: 29.3g; Carbohydrate: 30.9g; Fiber: 2.4g; Cholesterol: 62mg; Iron: 3.2mg; Sodium: 841mg; Calcium: 78mg

CHICKEN KEBABS AND NECTARINE SALSA Amount per serving (2 skewers and ¾ cup salsa): Calories: 324; Fat: 8.9g; Saturated fat: 1.5g; Monounsaturated fat: 4.9g; Polyunsaturated fat: 1.3g; Protein: 41.2g; Carbohydrate: 18.5g; Fiber: 3.8g; Cholesterol: 99mg; Iron: 1.9mg; Sodium: 547mg; Calcium: 44mg

GREEK CHICKEN BREAD SALAD Amount per serving (1⅓ cups salad and about 3 ounces chicken): Calories: 325; Fat: 14.2g; Saturated fat: 3.4g; Monounsaturated fat: 8.2g; Polyunsaturated fat: 1.5g; Protein: 30.5g; Carbohydrate: 18g; Fiber: 1.9g; Cholesterol: 75mg; Iron: 2.2mg; Sodium: 562mg; Calcium: 88mg

MAPLE-MUSTARD GLAZED CHICKEN Amount per serving (1 breast half and about 1 tablespoon sauce): Calories: 264; Fat: 4.4g; Saturated fat: 0.9g; Monounsaturated fat: 2.2g; Polyunsaturated fat: 0.7g; Protein: 39.5g; Carbohydrate: 14.2g; Fiber: 0.2g; Cholesterol: 99mg; Iron: 1.6mg; Sodium: 337mg; Calcium: 38mg

GRILLED CHICKEN FLORENTINE PASTA Amount per serving (about 1½ cups): Calories: 332; Fat: 10.3g; Saturated fat: 3.2g; Monounsaturated fat: 4.3g; Polyunsaturated fat: 1.7g; Protein: 24.8g; Carbohydrate: 35g; Fiber: 2g; Cholesterol: 46mg; Iron: 2.6mg; Sodium: 579mg; Calcium: 195mg

QUINOA SALAD WITH CHICKEN, AVOCADO, AND ORANGES Amount per serving (1½ cups): Calories: 490; Calories from fat: 48%; Protein: 21g; Fat: 26g; Saturated fat: 4.4g; Carbohydrate: 44g; Fiber: 10g; Sodium: 311mg; Cholesterol: 50mg

GRILLED CHICKEN SLIDERS AND APRICOT CHUTNEY SPREAD Amount per serving (2 sliders): Calories: 430; Fat: 11g; Saturated fat: 3.7g; Monounsaturated fat: 4.1g; Polyunsaturated fat: 1.7g; Protein: 42.3g; Carbohydrate: 41.9g; Fiber: 2.7g; Cholesterol: 141mg; Iron: 2mg; Sodium: 644mg; Calcium: 24mg

SPICY BASIL CHICKEN Amount per serving (¾ cup): Calories: 291; Fat: 15.2g; Saturated fat: 3.7g; Monounsaturated fat: 6.4g; Polyunsaturated fat: 3.6g; Protein: 31.3g; Carbohydrate: 5.6g; Fiber: 0.1g; Cholesterol: 112mg; Iron: 1.9mg; Sodium: 615mg; Calcium: 31mg

CHILI-LIME DRUMSTICKS Amount per serving (2 drumsticks): Calories: 294; Fat: 19g; Saturated fat: 7g; Protein: 28g; Carbohydrate: 2g; Fiber: 0g; Cholesterol: 134mg; Sodium: 277mg

CHICKEN IN WINE SAUCE Amount per serving (2 chicken thighs or ½ chicken breast half and about ½ cup sauce): Calories: 339; Fat: 9.8g; Saturated fat: 3.2g; Monounsaturated fat: 3.1g; Polyunsaturated fat: 1.6g; Protein: 35.8g; Carbohydrate: 11.4g; Fiber: 1.7g; Cholesterol: 116mg; Iron: 1.9mg; Sodium: 435mg; Calcium: 55mg

TURKEY SAUSAGE LASAGNA Amount per serving (¹⁄₁₀ of lasagna): Calories: 339; Fat: 14.7g; Saturated fat: 4.1g; Monounsaturated fat: 3.9g; Polyunsaturated fat: 0.7g; Protein: 24.2g; Carbohydrate: 29g; Fiber: 3.1g; Cholesterol: 87mg; Iron: 3.1mg; Sodium: 765mg; Calcium: 248mg

BEAN AND SAUSAGE STEW Amount per serving (¼ of stew): Calories: 495; Calories from fat: 28%; Fat: 14g; Saturated fat: 3g; Cholesterol: 65mg; Sodium: 1,020mg; Carbohydrate: 43g; Fiber: 9g; Sugars: 11g; Protein: 36g

TURKEY TENDERS Amount per serving (5 pieces): Calories: 227; Fat: 6.1g; Saturated fat: 1.2g; Monounsaturated fat: 2.7g; Polyunsaturated fat: 1.3g; Protein: 32.9g; Carbohydrate: 11g; Fiber: 0.5g; Cholesterol: 47mg; Iron: 2mg; Sodium: 237mg; Calcium: 36mg

SMOKE-ROASTED TURKEY BREAST WITH POMEGRANATE-THYME GLAZE Amount per serving (6 ounces turkey and about 1½ teaspoons sauce): Calories: 349; Fat: 2.2g; Saturated fat: 0.6g; Monounsaturated fat: 0.7g; Polyunsaturated fat: 0.5g; Protein: 64.3g; Carbohydrate: 14.3g; Fiber: 0.1g; Cholesterol: 176mg; Iron: 3.5mg; Sodium: 597mg; Calcium: 39mg

CASSOULET IN A FLASH Amount per serving (1 ramekin): Calories: 383; Fat: 21.7g; Saturated fat: 6.1g; Monounsaturated fat: 7.8g; Polyunsaturated fat: 5.7g; Protein: 20.7g; Carbohydrate: 26.9g; Fiber: 6.4g; Cholesterol: 66mg; Iron: 4.5mg; Sodium: 615mg; Calcium: 66mg

meats

CARAMELIZED ONION–AND–BLUE CHEESE MINI BURGERS Amount per serving (1 burger): Calories: 198; Fat: 6.6g; Saturated fat: 1.9g; Monounsaturated fat: 2.2g; Polyunsaturated fat: 1.4g; Protein: 16g; Carbohydrate: 20.5g; Fiber: 1.6g; Cholesterol: 32mg; Iron: 1.1mg; Sodium: 402mg; Calcium: 26mg

CHEESY MEAT LOAF MINIS Amount per serving (1 meat loaf): Calories: 254; Fat: 11.4g; Saturated fat: 5.8; Monounsaturated fat: 3.8g; Polyunsaturated fat: 0.9g; Protein: 28.3g; Carbohydrate: 11.1g; Fiber: 0.9g; Cholesterol: 112mg; Iron: 2.6mg; Sodium: 607mg; Calcium: 150mg

ENCHILADA CASSEROLE Amount per serving (1 wedge): Calories: 377; Fat: 14.6g; Saturated fat: 7g; Monounsaturated fat: 5.3g; Polyunsaturated fat: 1.6g; Protein: 30.2g; Carbohydrate: 32.4g; Fiber: 4.7g; Cholesterol: 76mg; Iron: 2.5mg; Sodium: 650mg; Calcium: 91mg

BEEF TENDERLOIN STEAKS AND BALSAMIC GREEN BEANS Amount per serving (1 steak and ½ cup bean mixture): Calories: 244; Fat: 9.4g; Saturated fat: 4g; Monounsaturated fat: 3.5g; Polyunsaturated fat: 0.4g; Protein: 27.1g; Carbohydrate: 12.4g; Fiber: 3.1g; Cholesterol: 81mg; Iron: 2.4mg; Sodium: 285mg; Calcium: 78mg

THAI BEEF SALAD Amount per serving (¼ of salad): Calories: 224; Protein: 20g; Fat: 11g; Saturated fat: 2.9g; Carbohydrate: 11g; Fiber: 0.8g; Sodium: 606mg; Cholesterol: 56mg

PAN-GRILLED FLANK STEAK WITH SOY-MUSTARD SAUCE Amount per serving (serving size: about 3 ounces steak and about 1 tablespoon sauce): Calories: 202; Fat: 9.7g; Saturated fat: 3.7g; Monounsaturated fat: 3.6g; Polyunsaturated fat: 0.6g; Protein: 25g; Carbohydrate: 2.3g; Fiber: 0g; Cholesterol: 45mg; Iron: 2mg; Sodium: 541mg; Calcium: 35mg

STIR-FRIED BEEF WITH NOODLES Amount per serving (¼ of recipe): Calories: 486; Fat: 15g; Saturated fat: 4g; Protein: 33g; Carbohydrate: 55g; Fiber: 4g; Cholesterol: 48mg; Sodium: 1359mg

BEEF AND GUINNESS STEW Amount per serving (1 cup): Calories: 365; Fat: 19.4g; Saturated fat: 5.7g; Monounsaturated fat: 9.6g; Polyunsaturated fat: 1.7g; Protein: 25.3g; Carbohydrate: 18.8g; Fiber: 3.6g; Cholesterol: 62mg; Iron: 2.6mg; Sodium: 454mg; Calcium: 52mg

PASTA PORK BOLOGNESE Amount per serving (1¼ cups): Calories: 412; Fat: 13.1g; Saturated fat: 4.6g; Monounsaturated fat: 5.1g; Polyunsaturated fat: 1g; Protein: 24.9g; Carbohydrate: 67.6g; Fiber: 2.1g; Cholesterol: 102mg; Iron: 1.7mg; Sodium: 468mg; Calcium: 35mg

GRILLED PORK CHOPS WITH TWO-MELON SALSA Amount per serving (1 pork chop and ½ cup salsa): Calories: 256; Fat: 13.5g; Saturated fat: 4.3g; Monounsaturated fat: 6.4g; Polyunsaturated fat: 1.6g; Protein: 25g; Carbohydrate: 8.7g; Fiber: 0.9g; Cholesterol: 70mg; Iron: 0.9mg; Sodium: 458mg

CUBAN SANDWICHES Amount per serving (1 sandwich): Calories: 397; Fat: 13.5g; Saturated fat: 4.4g; Monounsaturated fat: 4.6g; Polyunsaturated fat: 1.7g; Protein: 30.3g; Carbohydrate: 34.8g; Fiber: 1.8g; Cholesterol: 43mg; Iron: 2.9mg; Sodium: 984mg; Calcium: 398mg

PORK TENDERLOIN SALAD AND GRILLED NECTARINES Amount per serving (1½ cups salad, 3 ounces pork, and 5 nectarine wedges): Calories: 366; Fat: 19.8g; Saturated fat: 3.2g; Monounsaturated fat: 13.3g; Polyunsaturated fat: 2.3g; Protein: 25.9g; Carbohydrate: 22.7g; Fiber: 3.6g; Cholesterol: 74mg; Iron: 2.4mg; Sodium: 335mg; Calcium: 29mg

SPICED PORK TENDERLOIN WITH SAUTÉED APPLES Amount per serving (3 pork medallions and about ½ cup apple mixture): Calories: 234; Fat: 9.7g; Saturated fat: 5g; Monounsaturated fat: 3.2g; Polyunsaturated fat: 0.7g; Protein: 24.4g; Carbohydrate: 12.3g; Fiber: 1.5g; Cholesterol: 89mg; Iron: 1.7mg; Sodium: 394mg; Calcium: 18mg

GRILLED BABY BACK RIBS WITH STICKY BROWN SUGAR GLAZE Amount per serving (4 ribs plus ⅛ of glaze): Calories: 615; Protein: 33g; Fat: 41g; Saturated fat: 15g; Carbohydrate: 27g; Fiber: 0.1g; Sodium: 441mg; Cholesterol: 162mg

STICKY BROWN SUGAR GLAZE Amount per serving (⅛ of glaze): Calories: 106; Protein: 0g; Fat: 0g; Saturated fat: 0g; Carbohydrate: 27g; Fiber: 0g; Sodium: 11mg; Cholesterol: 0mg

INDIAN-SPICED LENTILS AND LAMB Amount per serving (1 cup lentils, 1 tablespoon yogurt, and 1 tablespoon cilantro): Calories: 371; Fat: 16g; Saturated fat: 7.1g; Monounsaturated fat: 5.8g; Polyunsaturated fat: 1.1g; Protein: 19.8g; Carbohydrate: 40.5g; Fiber: 9g; Cholesterol: 32mg; Iron: 4.3mg; Sodium: 619mg; Calcium: 107mg

GREEK LAMB CHOPS AND MINT YOGURT SAUCE Amount per serving (2 lamb chops and 2 tablespoons sauce): Calories: 347; Fat: 14g; Saturated fat: 4.2g; Monounsaturated fat: 6.2g; Polyunsaturated fat: 1.3g; Protein: 48.2g; Carbohydrate: 3.9g; Fiber: 0g; Cholesterol: 147mg; Iron: 4.5mg; Sodium: 347mg; Calcium: 86mg

ROAST LEG OF LAMB WITH CHILE-GARLIC SAUCE Amount per serving (3 ounces lamb and about 1 tablespoon sauce): Calories: 265; Fat: 18.5g; Saturated fat: 6.3g; Monounsaturated fat: 9.7g; Polyunsaturated fat: 1.2g; Protein: 21.7g; Carbohydrate: 1.8g; Fiber: 0.2g; Cholesterol: 71mg; Iron: 2mg; Sodium: 574mg; Calcium: 17mg

fish & shellfish

OPEN-FACED BLACKENED CATFISH SANDWICHES Amount per serving (1 sandwich): Calories: 362; Fat: 16g; Saturated fat: 3.4g; Monounsaturated fat: 7.8g; Polyunsaturated fat: 3.2g; Protein: 31.3g; Carbohydrate: 22.6g; Fiber: 2.2g; Cholesterol: 80mg; Iron: 2.4mg; Sodium: 414mg; Calcium: 63mg

ARCTIC CHAR AND VEGETABLES IN PARCHMENT HEARTS Amount per serving (1 fillet, ½ cup vegetables, and about 1 tablespoon sauce): Calories: 301; Fat: 14.6g; Saturated fat: 6.4g; Monounsaturated fat: 3.8g; Polyunsaturated fat: 2.7g; Protein: 34.8g; Carbohydrate: 6g; Fiber: 1.4g; Cholesterol: 111mg; Iron: 1.8mg; Sodium: 369mg; Calcium: 45mg

CHIP-CRUSTED FISH FILLETS Amount per serving (serving size: 1 fillet and 2 tablespoons ranch dressing): Calories: 291; Fat: 11.3g; Saturated fat: 1.2g; Monounsaturated fat: 5.7g; Polyunsaturated fat: 2.8g; Protein: 31.7g; Carbohydrate: 14.5g; Fiber: 0.8g; Cholesterol: 79mg; Iron: 1.4mg; Sodium: 549mg; Calcium: 49mg

PAN-SEARED GROUPER WITH ROMAINE SLAW Amount per serving (1 fillet and ¼ of slaw): Calories: 501; Fat: 21g; Saturated fat: 3.6g; Protein: 29mg; Carbohydrate: 42g; Fiber: 7.5g; Cholesterol: 63mg; Iron: 5mg; Sodium: 682mg; Calcium: 165mg

HALIBUT WITH SMOKY ORANGE VINAIGRETTE Amount per serving (¼ of recipe): Calories: 486; Fat: 15g; Saturated fat: 4g; Protein: 33g; Carbohydrate: 55g; Fiber: 4g; Cholesterol: 48mg; Sodium: 1359mg

CEDAR PLANK-GRILLED SALMON WITH MANGO KIWI SALSA Amount per serving (1 fillet and ⅓ cup salsa): Calories: 267; Fat: 7.5g; Saturated fat: 1.2g; Monounsaturated fat: 2.5g; Polyunsaturated fat: 2.6g; Protein: 34.7g; Carbohydrate: 14.8g; Fiber: 2.2g; Cholesterol: 88mg; Iron: 1.6mg; Sodium: 356mg; Calcium: 42mg

TILAPIA PICCATA Amount per serving (1 fillet and ¼ of sauce): Calories: 414; Fat: 21g; Saturated fat: 8g; Protein: 43g; Carbohydrate: 8g; Fiber: 0g; Cholesterol: 133mg; Sodium: 479mg

SESAME TUNA WITH EDAMAME AND SOBA Amount per serving (1 tuna steak and ¾ cup noodles): Calories: 413; Fat: 11.8g; Saturated fat: 1.4g; Monounsaturated fat: 4.1g; Polyunsaturated fat: 3.7g; Protein: 50.2g; Carbohydrate: 26.7g; Fiber: 2.6g; Cholesterol: 77mg; Iron: 4.1mg; Sodium: 606mg; Calcium: 103mg

TUNA NIÇOISE SALAD WITH ROASTED GREEN BEANS AND POTATOES Amount per serving (4 cups salad and 1½ tablespoons dressing): Calories: 365; Fat: 23.2g; Saturated fat: 4.1g; Monounsaturated fat: 11.3g; Polyunsaturated fat: 3.7g; Protein: 20g; Carbohydrate: 20g; Fiber: 4g; Cholesterol: 206mg; Iron: 3mg; Sodium: 617mg; Calcium: 88mg

CRAB CAKES WITH SPICY RÉMOULADE Amount per serving (2 crab cakes and about 1 tablespoon sauce): Calories: 160; Fat: 8.5g; Saturated fat: 0.6g; Monounsaturated fat: 4.4g; Polyunsaturated fat: 2.5g; Protein: 13.4g; Carbohydrate: 5.9g; Fiber: 0.5g; Cholesterol: 83mg; Iron: 0.8mg; Sodium: 273mg; Calcium: 67mg

SIMPLE LOBSTER RISOTTO Amount per serving (1 cup): Calories: 374; Fat: 10.7g; Saturated fat: 5.8g; Monounsaturated fat: 2.6g; Polyunsaturated fat: 0.9g; Protein: 24.7g; Carbohydrate: 44.4g; Fiber: 4.1g; Cholesterol: 80mg; Iron: 2mg; Sodium: 620mg; Calcium: 63mg

SEARED SCALLOPS WITH BACON, CABBAGE, AND APPLE Amount per serving (1 cup cabbage mixture, 4 scallops, and ½ teaspoon dill): Calories: 201; Fat: 6.1g; Saturated fat: 2.8g; Monounsaturated fat: 2.3g; Polyunsaturated fat: 1.3g; Protein: 22.4g; Carbohydrate: 15.1g; Fiber: 3.9g; Cholesterol: 43mg; Iron: 1.2mg; Sodium: 458mg; Calcium: 86mg

SPICY SHRIMP NOODLE SOUP Amount per serving (½ cup noodles and about 1 cup soup): Calories: 287; Fat: 2.1g; Saturated fat: 0.4g; Monounsaturated fat: 0.3g; Polyunsaturated fat: 0.8g; Protein: 26.7g; Carbohydrate: 40.3g; Fiber: 4g; Cholesterol: 174mg; Iron: 11.1mg; Sodium: 537mg; Calcium: 96mg

MANGO AVOCADO SHRIMP SALAD Amount per serving (⅙ of salad): Calories: 288; Calories from fat: 44%; Protein: 18g; Fat: 14g; Saturated fat: 2.1g; Carbohydrate: 26g; Fiber: 2.6g; Sodium: 180mg; Cholesterol: 148mg

meatless mains

GRILLED VEGGIE AND HUMMUS WRAPS Amount per serving (1 wrap): Calories: 356; Fat: 22.7g; Saturated fat: 3.1g; Monounsaturated fat: 13.6g; Polyunsaturated fat: 4.4g; Protein: 16.8g; Carbohydrate: 35.4g; Fiber: 15.3g; Cholesterol: 13mg; Iron: 3.6mg; Sodium: 788mg; Calcium: 156mg

EGGPLANT PARMESAN PIZZA Amount per serving (1 slice): Calories: 337; Fat: 8g

GRILLED STUFFED PORTOBELLO MUSHROOMS Amount per serving (1 mushroom cap): Calories: 216; Fat: 8.6g; Saturated fat: 2.7g; Monounsaturated fat: 4.1g; Polyunsaturated fat: 1g; Protein: 10g; Carbohydrate: 25g; Fiber: 3.2g; Cholesterol: 9mg; Iron: 1mg; Sodium: 300mg; Calcium: 146mg

SPINACH PIE WITH GOAT CHEESE, RAISINS, AND PINE NUTS Amount per serving (1 piece): Calories: 363; Fat: 21.8g; Saturated fat: 6.6g; Monounsaturated fat: 9.9g; Polyunsaturated fat: 3.6g; Protein: 14.9g; Carbohydrate: 31.9g; Fiber: 6.4g; Cholesterol: 13mg; Iron: 5.3mg; Sodium: 480mg; Calcium: 300mg

FRESH TOMATO BASIL PIZZA Calories: 144; Fat: 5.8g; Saturated fat: 1.1g; Protein: 3.6g; Carbohydrate: 20g; Fiber: 1.2g; Sodium: 242mg

LENTIL-BARLEY BURGERS WITH FIERY FRUIT SALSA Amount per serving (2 patties and ¼ cup salsa): Calories: 315; Fat: 12.8g; Saturated fat: 1.2g; Monounsaturated fat: 6.8g; Polyunsaturated fat: 3.5g; Protein: 12.8g; Carbohydrate: 39.2g; Fiber: 9.5g; Cholesterol: 53mg; Iron: 3.9mg; Sodium: 539mg; Calcium: 60mg

RED QUINOA SALAD Amount per serving (about 1¾ cups salad and 1 lemon wedge) Calories: 460; Fat: 24.7g; Saturated fat: 5g; Monounsaturated fat: 14.7g; Polyunsaturated fat: 3.8g; Protein: 12.5g; Carbohydrate: 48.4g; Fiber: 7.4g; Cholesterol: 13mg; Iron: 3.5mg; Sodium: 499mg; Calcium: 133mg

CREAMY SPRING PASTA Amount per serving (about 1¼ cups): Calories: 408; Fat: 13.8g; Saturated fat: 6.7g; Monounsaturated fat: 4.5g; Polyunsaturated fat: 1.1g; Protein: 17.6g; Carbohydrate: 54g; Fiber: 4.6g; Cholesterol: 33mg; Iron: 3.9mg; Sodium: 625mg; Calcium: 225mg

TORTELLINI WITH PEAS AND TARRAGON Amount per serving (¼ of pasta): Calories: 474; Fat: 22g; Saturated fat: 8g; Cholesterol: 41mg; Sodium: 730mg; Carbohydrate: 50g; Fiber: 4g; Sugars: 5g; Protein: 17g

BROWNED BUTTER GNOCCHI WITH BROCCOLI AND NUTS Amount per serving (1½ cups gnocchi mixture, 1½ teaspoons pine nuts, and about 2 teaspoons cheese): Calories: 368; Fat: 12.8g; Saturated fat: 3.8g; Monounsaturated fat: 5.1g; Polyunsaturated fat: 2.2g; Protein: 7.9g; Carbohydrate: 56.6g; Fiber: 5.7g; Cholesterol: 13mg; Iron: 1.2mg; Sodium: 614mg; Calcium: 104mg

CREAMY FOUR-CHEESE MACARONI Amount per serving (1 cup): Calories: 347; Fat: 11.5g; Saturated fat: 5.9g; Monounsaturated fat: 3.4g; Polyunsaturated fat: 1.4g; Protein: 17.4g; Carbohydrate: 43.8g; Fiber: 19g; Cholesterol: 29mg; Iron: 1.7mg; Sodium: 607mg; Calcium: 346mg

CHICKPEAS IN CURRIED COCONUT BROTH Amount per serving (1⅓ cups chickpea mixture and 1 cup rice): Calories: 369; Calories from fat: 0%; Fat: 4.3g; Saturated fat: 0.9g; Monounsaturated fat: 1.4g; Polyunsaturated fat: 1.1g; Protein: 10.5g; Carbohydrate: 71.1g; Fiber: 6.4g; Cholesterol: 0mg; Iron: 4mg; Sodium: 620mg; Calcium: 55mg

CHEESY CORN-AND-BLACK-BEAN QUESADILLAS Amount per serving (6 wedges): Calories: 305; Fat: 12g; Saturated fat: 6g; Protein: 12g; Carbohydrate: 40g; Fiber: 5g; Cholesterol: 19mg; Sodium: 789mg

GINGERY BUTTERNUT SQUASH AND TOFU CURRY Amount per serving (1½ cups curry and ¾ cup rice): Calories: 291; Fat: 8g; Saturated fat: 2g; Monounsaturated fat: 2g; Polyunsaturated fat: 2g; Protein: 13g; Carbohydrate: 44g; Fiber: 6g; Cholesterol: 3mg; Iron: 3mg; Sodium: 250mg; Calcium: 377mg

VEGGIE AND TOFU STIR-FRY Amount per serving (1½ cups): Calories: 233; Fat: 11.8g; Saturated fat: 1.8g; Monounsaturated fat: 3.9g; Polyunsaturated fat: 5.2g; Protein: 12.9g; Carbohydrate: 17.5g; Fiber: 3.2g; Cholesterol: 0mg; Iron: 3mg; Sodium: 389mg; Calcium: 227mg

TOFU STEAKS WITH SHIITAKES AND VEGGIES Amount per serving (1 tofu steak, about ⅓ cup carrot mixture, and about 2 tablespoons mushroom mixture): Calories: 268; Fat: 16.5g; Saturated fat: 2.7g; Monounsaturated fat: 5.3g; Polyunsaturated fat: 7.9g; Protein: 11.4g; Carbohydrate: 19g; Fiber: 2.2g; Cholesterol: 0mg; Iron: 1.8mg; Sodium: 462mg; Calcium: 91mg

LETTUCE WRAPS WITH HOISIN-PEANUT SAUCE Amount per serving (2 lettuce wraps and 2 tablespoons sauce): Calories: 355; Fat: 15g; Saturated fat: 2.1g; Monounsaturated fat: 8.5g; Polyunsaturated fat: 3.7g; Protein: 16.2g; Carbohydrate: 42.6g; Fiber: 3.9g; Cholesterol: 0mg; Iron: 4.5mg; Sodium: 568mg; Calcium: 224mg

ZUCCHINI AND CARAMELIZED ONION QUICHE Amount per serving (1 wedge): Calories: 314; Fat: 18.1g; Saturated fat: 6.2g; Monounsaturated fat: 7.5g; Polyunsaturated fat: 3.1g; Protein: 9.6g; Carbohydrate: 28.5g; Fiber: 1.9g; Cholesterol: 119mg; Iron: 1.1mg; Sodium: 564mg; Calcium: 164mg

BASIC CARAMELIZED ONIONS Amount per serving (¼ cup): Calories: 126; Fat: 6.7g; Saturated fat: 1.7g; Monounsaturated fat: 4.1g; Polyunsaturated fat: 0.6g; Protein: 1.9g; Carbohydrate: 16.1g; Fiber: 2.9g; Cholesterol: 4mg; Iron: 0.4mg; Sodium: 77mg; Calcium: 40mg

vegetable sides & salads

ARUGULA AVOCADO SALAD Amount per serving (¼ of salad): Calories: 241; Protein: 5.4g; Fat: 23g; Saturated fat: 3.7g; Carbohydrate: 7.9g; Fiber: 2.6g; Sodium: 174mg; Cholesterol: 16mg

GRILLED ASPARAGUS WITH CAPER VINAIGRETTE Amount per serving (about 4 asparagus spears and about 2 teaspoons vinaigrette): Calories: 91; Fat: 7.2g; Saturated fat: 1.1g; Monounsaturated fat: 5g; Polyunsaturated fat: 1.1g; Protein: 2.6g; Carbohydrate: 4.8g; Fiber: 2.5g; Cholesterol: 0mg; Iron: 2.5mg; Sodium: 198mg; Calcium: 32mg

SIMPLE SESAME SALAD Amount per serving (about 1⅓ cups): Calories: 83; Fat: 7.1g; Saturated fat: 1g; Monounsaturated fat: 2.8g; Polyunsaturated fat: 3.1g; Protein: 1.8g; Carbohydrate: 4.9g; Fiber: 2.5g; Cholesterol: 0mg; Iron: 1.1mg; Sodium: 177mg; Calcium: 32mg

BUTTERY LEMON BROCCOLINI Amount per serving (3 ounces Broccolini and about 1 teaspoon butter mixture): Calories: 61; Fat: 2.8g; Saturated fat: 1.8g; Monounsaturated fat: 0.7g; Polyunsaturated fat: 0.1g; Protein: 3.1g; Carbohydrate: 6.3g; Fiber: 1.1g; Cholesterol: 8mg; Iron: 0.7mg; Sodium: 176mg; Calcium: 62mg

BROCCOLI RABE WITH GARLIC AND GOLDEN RAISINS Amount per serving (about ⅔ cup): Calories: 95; Fat: 3.4g; Saturated fat: 0.5g; Monounsaturated fat: 2.5g; Polyunsaturated fat: 0.4g; Protein: 4.5g; Carbohydrate: 13.4g; Fiber: 0.5g; Cholesterol: 0mg; Iron: 1.2mg; Sodium: 155mg; Calcium: 63mg

STEAMED CARROTS WITH GARLIC-GINGER BUTTER Amount per serving (¼ of carrots): Calories: 69; Fat: 3g; Saturated fat: 1.8g; Monounsaturated fat: 0.8g; Polyunsaturated fat: 0.2g; Protein: 0.9g; Carbohydrate: 10.3g; Fiber: 3.4g; Cholesterol: 8mg; Iron: 1.1mg; Sodium: 257mg; Calcium: 41mg

CREAMY LIME SLAW Amount per serving (⅛ of slaw): Calories: 49; Fat: 2.9g; Protein: 0.1g; Saturated fat: 0g; Carbohydrate: 9.5g; Fiber: 2.2g; Sodium: 268mg; Cholesterol: 0mg

CURRIED CAULIFLOWER WITH CAPERS Amount per serving (about 1 cup): Calories: 107; Fat: 9.5g; Saturated fat: 1.3g; Monounsaturated fat: 6.6g; Polyunsaturated fat: 1.2g; Protein: 2.1g; Carbohydrate: 5.3g; Fiber: 2.6g; Cholesterol: 0mg; Iron: 0.7mg; Sodium: 445mg; Calcium: 24mg

BALSAMIC COLLARD GREENS Amount per serving (½ cup collard greens and 2½ teaspoons bacon): Calories: 82; Fat: 1.8g; Saturated fat: 0.8g; Monounsaturated fat: 0.8g; Polyunsaturated fat: 0.4g; Protein: 5g; Carbohydrate: 13.6g; Fiber: 3.8g; Cholesterol: 6mg; Iron: 0.3mg; Sodium: 260mg; Calcium: 144mg

GRILLED CORN POBLANO SALAD WITH CHIPOTLE VINAIGRETTE Amount per serving (½ cup): Calories: 283; Protein: 5.7g; Fat: 11g; Saturated fat: 1.2g; Carbohydrate: 43g; Fiber: 1.7g; Sodium: 171mg; Cholesterol: 0mg

ROASTED SQUASH AND KALE SALAD Amount per serving (1½ cups): Calories: 299; Fat: 14g; Saturated fat: 2g; Monounsaturated fat: 3g; Polyunsaturated fat: 3g; Protein: 8g; Carbohydrate: 42g; Fiber: 8g; Cholesterol: 0mg; Iron: 3mg; Sodium: 325mg; Calcium: 237mg

GARLIC-ROASTED KALE Amount per serving (about ⅔ cup): Calories: 72; Fat: 4.7g; Saturated fat: 0.7g; Monounsaturated fat: 3g; Polyunsaturated fat: 0.8g; Protein: 2.3g; Carbohydrate: 7.1g; Fiber: 1.4g; Cholesterol: 0mg; Iron: 1.2mg; Sodium: 125mg; Calcium: 93mg

SUMMER SQUASH RIBBONS WITH LEMON AND PARMESAN Amount per serving (¼ of squash): Calories: 149; Protein: 8g; Carbohydrate: 6g; Sugars: 3g; Fiber: 2g; Fat: 11g; Saturated fat: 3g; Sodium: 503mg; Cholesterol: 10mg

LEMON-GARLIC SWISS CHARD Amount per serving (about ½ cup): Calories: 61; Fat: 4.1g; Saturated fat: 0.8g; Monounsaturated fat: 2.7g; Polyunsaturated fat: 0.5g; Protein: 2.7g; Carbohydrate: 5g; Fiber: 1.8g; Cholesterol: 1mg; Iron: 2mg; Sodium: 256mg; Calcium: 78mg

MOZZARELLA, TOMATO, AND BASIL SALAD Amount per serving (⅛ of salad): Calories: 277; Fat: 19g; Saturated fat: 11g; Protein: 20g; Carbohydrate: 7g; Fiber: 2g; Cholesterol: 66mg; Sodium: 123mg

EVERYDAY ROAST VEGETABLES Amount per serving (about 1¼ cups): Calories: 225; Fat: 10.8g; Saturated fat: 1.5g; Monounsaturated fat: 7.5g; Polyunsaturated fat: 1.3g; Protein: 4g; Carbohydrate: 31g; Fiber: 8g; Cholesterol: 0mg; Iron: 2mg; Sodium: 720mg; Calcium: 77mg

GRILLED ZUCCHINI WITH SEA SALT Amount per serving (about 4 slices): Calories: 36; Fat: 2.4g; Saturated fat: 0.4g; Monounsaturated fat: 1.7g; Polyunsaturated fat: 0.3g; Protein: 1.2g; Carbohydrate: 3.4g; Fiber: 1.1g; Cholesterol: 0mg; Iron: 0.4mg; Sodium: 130mg; Calcium: 15mg

LAVENDER-SCENTED SUMMER FRUIT SALAD Amount per serving (1¼ cups): Calories: 119; Fat: 1g; Saturated fat: 0g; Monounsaturated fat: 0g; Polyunsaturated fat: 0g; Protein: 2g; Carbohydrate: 30g; Fiber: 6g; Cholesterol: 0mg; Iron: 1mg; Sodium: 37mg; Calcium: 26mg

NEW-FASHIONED APPLE AND RAISIN SLAW Amount per serving (1 cup): Calories: 120; Fat: 2.2g; Saturated fat: 1.2g; Monounsaturated fat: 0.8g; Polyunsaturated fat: 0.2g; Protein: 2.3g; Carbohydrate: 25.3g; Fiber: 3.3g; Cholesterol: 0mg; Iron: 0.8mg; Sodium: 162mg; Calcium: 31mg

MELON BALL SALAD WITH LIME SYRUP Amount per serving (⅛ of salad): Calories: 269; Fat: 1g; Saturated fat: 0g; Protein: 4g; Carbohydrate: 68g; Fiber: 4g; Cholesterol: 0mg; Sodium: 75mg

bean, grain & potato sides

CREAMY CANNELLINI BEANS WITH GARLIC AND OREGANO Amount per serving (½ cup): Calories: 231; Fat: 6.8g; Saturated fat: 0.9g; Monounsaturated fat: 4.9g; Polyunsaturated fat: 0.7g; Protein: 12.1g; Carbohydrate: 30.3g; Fiber: 8g; Cholesterol: 0mg; Iron: 5.5mg; Sodium: 310mg; Calcium: 102mg

EDAMAME SALAD Amount per serving (⅛ of salad): Calories: 113; Protein: 6.6g; Fat: 7.6g; Saturated fat: 0.6g; Carbohydrate: 6.2g; Fiber: 3.2g; Sodium: 93mg; Cholesterol: 0mg

BULGUR WHEAT SALAD WITH TOMATO AND EGGPLANT Amount per serving (¼ of salad): Calories: 319; Protein: 7g; Carbohydrate: 38g; Sugars: 6g; Fiber: 12g; Fat: 18g; Saturated fat: 2g; Sodium: 255mg; Cholesterol: 0mg

SAUSAGE AND SOURDOUGH BREAD STUFFING Amount per serving (about ¾ cup): Calories: 149; Fat: 6.3g; Saturated fat: 1.8g; Monounsaturated fat: 1g; Polyunsaturated fat: 0.5g; Protein: 7.2g; Carbohydrate: 15.9g; Fiber: 1.3g; Cholesterol: 34mg; Iron: 1.6mg; Sodium: 396mg; Calcium: 61mg

HERBED COUSCOUS PILAF Amount per serving (¾ cup): Calories: 205; Fat: 3.7g; Saturated fat: 0.5g; Monounsaturated fat: 2.5g; Polyunsaturated fat: 0.5g; Protein: 6.5g; Carbohydrate: 35.6g; Fiber: 2.6g; Cholesterol: 0mg; Iron: 0.8mg; Sodium: 189mg; Calcium: 20mg

QUINOA WITH ROASTED GARLIC, TOMATOES, AND SPINACH Amount per serving (½ cup): Calories: 130; Fat: 5g; Saturated fat: 0.7g; Monounsaturated fat: 3.1g; Polyunsaturated fat: 1g; Protein: 4.1g; Carbohydrate: 16.6g; Fiber: 1.8g; Cholesterol: 1mg; Iron: 1.7mg; Sodium: 305mg; Calcium: 49mg

BROWN RICE PILAF WITH ALMONDS AND PARSLEY Amount per serving (¾ cup): Calories: 261; Fat: 8g; Saturated fat: 1g; Cholesterol: 0mg; Sodium: 246mg; Carbohydrate: 42g; Fiber: 4g; Sugars: 2g; Protein: 6g

HOME FRIES Amount per serving (about ¾ cup): Calories: 248; Fat: 9.8g; Saturated fat: 2.9g; Monounsaturated fat: 4.7g; Polyunsaturated fat: 1.8g; Protein: 4.8g; Carbohydrate: 35.4g; Fiber: 3.3g; Cholesterol: 10mg; Iron: 1.7mg; Sodium: 201mg; Calcium: 29mg

LOADED TWICE-BAKED POTATOES Amount per serving (1 potato half): Calories: 194; Fat: 12.7g; Saturated fat: 1.2g; Monounsaturated fat: 0.6g; Polyunsaturated fat: 0.1g; Protein: 4.9g; Carbohydrate: 15.8g; Fiber: 1.9g; Cholesterol: 7mg; Iron: 1mg; Sodium: 193mg; Calcium: 126mg

OVEN ROASTED SWEET POTATO CHIPS WITH RANCH DIP Amount per serving (about 11 chips with 1 tablespoon dip): Calories: 194; Fat: 6g

ROSEMARY MASHED SWEET POTATOES WITH SHALLOTS Amount per serving (about ½ cup): Calories: 202; Fat: 6.3g; Saturated fat: 0.9g; Monounsaturated fat: 4.5g; Polyunsaturated fat: 0.9g; Protein: 2.9g; Carbohydrate: 34.9g; Fiber: 4.8g; Cholesterol: 0mg; Iron: 1.2mg; Sodium: 278mg; Calcium: 55mg

ROASTED SWEET POTATOES AND APPLES Amount per serving (¹⁄₁₀ of dish): Calories: 151; Protein: 1.5g; Fat: 3.5g; Saturated fat: 0.5g; Carbohydrate: 30g; Fiber: 3.7g; Sodium: 286mg; Cholesterol: 0mg

desserts

CHEWY CARAMEL APPLE COOKIES Amount per serving (1 cookie): Calories: 115; Fat: 4g; Saturated fat: 2.3g; Monounsaturated fat: 1g; Polyunsaturated fat: 0.3g; Protein: 1.6g; Carbohydrate: 18.4g; Fiber: 1g; Cholesterol: 15mg; Iron: 0.4mg; Sodium: 61mg; Calcium: 22mg

ROASTED BANANA BARS WITH BROWNED BUTTER–PECAN FROSTING Amount per serving (1 bar): Calories: 221; Fat: 8.4g; Saturated fat: 4.7g; Monounsaturated fat: 2.3g; Polyunsaturated fat: 0.6g; Protein: 2.3g; Carbohydrate: 35.1g; Fiber: 0.6g; Cholesterol: 39mg; Iron: 1mg; Sodium: 117mg; Calcium: 23mg

HONEYED APPLES WITH ICE CREAM Amount per serving (⅙ of recipe): Calories: 316; Fat: 18g; Saturated fat: 11g; Protein: 4g; Carbohydrate: 37g; Fiber: 1g; Cholesterol: 95mg; Sodium: 48mg

CHERRY-ALMOND CRISP Amount per serving (about ⅔ cup crisp): Calories: 277; Fat: 7g; Saturated fat: 3.3g; Monounsaturated fat: 2.2g; Polyunsaturated fat: 0.8g; Protein: 3.3g; Carbohydrate: 52.2g; Fiber: 5.5g; Cholesterol: 13mg; Iron: 1.5mg; Sodium: 103mg; Calcium: 36mg

RED VELVET CUPCAKES Amount per serving (1 cupcake): Calories: 205; Fat: 7.3g; Saturated fat: 4.5g; Monounsaturated fat: 2g; Polyunsaturated fat: 0.3g; Protein: 2.3g; Carbohydrate: 33.5g; Fiber: 0.3g; Cholesterol: 34mg; Iron: 0.9mg; Sodium: 168mg; Calcium: 35mg

GRILLED POUND CAKE WITH LEMON CREAM AND BLUEBERRIES Amount per serving (⅛ of recipe): Calories: 205; Fat: 12g; Saturated fat: 7g; Protein: 2g; Carbohydrate: 23g; Fiber: 1g; Cholesterol: 91mg; Sodium: 124mg

WHITE AND DARK CHOCOLATE PUDDING PARFAITS Amount per serving (1 parfait): Calories: 574; Fat: 37g; Saturated fat: 22g; Protein: 8g; Carbohydrate: 61g; Fiber: 8g; Cholesterol: 96mg; Sodium: 128mg

TART LEMON ICE WITH CRUSHED STRAWBERRIES Amount per serving (½ cup lemon ice and 2 tablespoons strawberry mixture): Calories: 133; Fat: 0.1g; Polyunsaturated fat: 0.1g; Protein: 0.4g; Carbohydrate: 35g; Fiber: 0.8g; Cholesterol: 0mg; Iron: 0.2mg; Sodium: 1mg; Calcium: 9mg

LAST-MINUTE TROPICAL SHERBET Amount per serving (¾ cup): Calories: 144; Fat: 0.6g; Saturated fat: 0.4g; Monounsaturated fat: 0.2g; Polyunsaturated fat: 0g; Protein: 3g; Carbohydrate: 34.1g; Fiber: 2.5g; Cholesterol: 2mg; Iron: 0.3mg; Sodium: 78mg; Calcium: 29mg

STRAWBERRY-RHUBARB ICE CREAM Amount per serving (¾ cup): Calories: 173; Fat: 5.6g; Saturated fat: 2.9g; Monounsaturated fat: 1.7g; Polyunsaturated fat: 0.5g; Protein: 3.8g; Carbohydrate: 28.2g; Fiber: 1.3g; Cholesterol: 74mg; Iron: 0.4mg; Sodium: 123mg; Calcium: 123mg

PEANUT BUTTER ICE CREAM SANDWICHES Amount per serving (1 sandwich): Calories: 410; Fat: 23g; Saturated fat: 10g; Protein: 9g; Carbohydrate: 42g; Fiber: 2g; Cholesterol: 53mg; Sodium: 101mg

METRIC EQUIVALENTS

The recipes that appear in this cookbook use the standard U.S. method for measuring liquid and dry or solid ingredients (teaspoons, tablespoons, and cups). The information in the following charts is provided to help cooks outside the United States successfully use these recipes. All equivalents are approximate.

Metric Equivalents for Different Types of Ingredients

A standard cup measure of a dry or solid ingredient will vary in weight depending on the type of ingredient. A standard cup of liquid is the same volume for any type of liquid. Use the following chart when converting standard cup measures to grams (weight) or milliliters (volume).

Standard Cup	Fine Powder (ex. flour)	Grain (ex. rice)	Granular (ex. sugar)	Liquid Solids (ex. butter)	Liquid (ex. milk)
1	140 g	150 g	190 g	200 g	240 ml
¾	105 g	113 g	143 g	150 g	180 ml
⅔	93 g	100 g	125 g	133 g	160 ml
½	70 g	75 g	95 g	100 g	120 ml
⅓	47 g	50 g	63 g	67 g	80 ml
¼	35 g	38 g	48 g	50 g	60 ml
⅛	18 g	19 g	24 g	25 g	30 ml

Useful Equivalents for Liquid Ingredients by Volume

¼ tsp					=	1 ml
½ tsp					=	2 ml
1 tsp					=	5 ml
3 tsp	=	1 Tbsp		= ½ fl oz	=	15 ml
		2 Tbsp	= ⅛ cup	= 1 fl oz	=	30 ml
		4 Tbsp	= ¼ cup	= 2 fl oz	=	60 ml
		5⅓ Tbsp	= ⅓ cup	= 3 fl oz	=	80 ml
		8 Tbsp	= ½ cup	= 4 fl oz	=	120 ml
		10⅔ Tbsp	= ⅔ cup	= 5 fl oz	=	160 ml
		12 Tbsp	= ¾ cup	= 6 fl oz	=	180 ml
		16 Tbsp	= 1 cup	= 8 fl oz	=	240 ml
		1 pt	= 2 cups	= 16 fl oz	=	480 ml
		1 qt	= 4 cups	= 32 fl oz	=	960 ml
				33 fl oz	=	1000 ml	= 1 l

Useful Equivalents for Dry Ingredients by Weight

(To convert ounces to grams, multiply the number of ounces by 30.)

1 oz	=	¹⁄₁₆ lb	=	30 g
4 oz	=	¼ lb	=	120 g
8 oz	=	½ lb	=	240 g
12 oz	=	¾ lb	=	360 g
16 oz	=	1 lb	=	480 g

Useful Equivalents for Length

(To convert inches to centimeters, multiply the number of inches by 2.5.)

1 in				=	2.5 cm		
6 in	=	½ ft		=	15 cm		
12 in	=	1 ft		=	30 cm		
36 in	=	3 ft	= 1 yd	=	90 cm		
40 in				=	100 cm	= 1 m

Useful Equivalents for Cooking/Oven Temperatures

	Fahrenheit	Celsius	Gas Mark
Freeze water	32° F	0° C	
Room temperature	68° F	20° C	
Boil water	212° F	100° C	
Bake	325° F	160° C	3
	350° F	180° C	4
	375° F	190° C	5
	400° F	200° C	6
	425° F	220° C	7
	450° F	230° C	8
Broil			Grill

INDEX

ACKNOWLEDGMENTS

Photographers: Jean Allsopp, 83; Johnny Autry, 18, 21, 22, 26, 27, 37, 47, 52, 53, 59, 60, 64, 65, 84, 87, 89, 95, 97, 105, 109, 111, 131, 133, 144, 146, 155, 161, 178, 182, 196, 200; Iain Bagwell, 13, 42, 73, 76, 114, 156, 175, 192, 222, 241; Leigh Beisch, 210; Ryan Benyi, 28, 236, 247; Annabelle Breakey, 24; Levi Brown, 135; Maren Caruso, 125; Nigel Cox, 245; Jennifer Davick, 32, 55, 92, 101, 140, 142, 159, 170, 171, 197, 199, 217, 221, 225, 228, 234, 242; William Dickey, 162; Jim Franco, 233, 239; Dan Goldberg, 154; Leo Gong, 51; Alexandra Grablewski, 54, 96; Beth Dreiling Hontzas, 216; José Picayo, 58, 118, 205; Howard L. Puckett, 184; Lisa Romerein, 169; Kate Sears, 185, 232; Mary Britton Senseney, 23; Ellen Silverman, 160; Becky Luigart-Stayner, 11, 15, 63, 79, 93, 106, 110, 126, 166, 218, 231, 246; Mark Thomas, 139, 179; Luca Trovato, 112; Jonny Valiant, 57, 174, 195, 209; Anna Williams, 226; Brian Woodcock, 31

ISBN-13: 978-0-8487-4227-0
ISBN-10: 0-8487-4227-3
Library of Congress Control Number: 2013941647

Printed in the United States of America
First Printing 2013

Oxmoor House

Editorial Director: Leah McLaughlin
Creative Director: Felicity Keane
Brand Manager: Vanessa Tiongson
Senior Editors: Heather Averett, Rebecca Brennan
Managing Editor: Elizabeth Tyler Austin

MyRecipes Easy Meal Maker

Editor: Nichole Aksamit
Art Director: Claire Cormany
Project Editor: Lacie Pinyan
Assistant Designer: Allison Sperando Potter
Assistant Directors, Test Kitchen: Julie Christopher,
    Julie Gunter
Recipe Developers and Testers: Wendy Ball, R.D., Victoria E. Cox,
    Tamara Goldis, Stefanie Maloney, Callie Nash, Karen Rankin,
    Leah Van Deren
Recipe Editor: Alyson Moreland Haynes
Food Stylists: Margaret Monroe Dickey, Catherine Crowell Steele
Photography Director: Jim Bathie
Senior Photographer: Hélène Dujardin
Senior Photo Stylist: Kay E. Clarke
Photo Stylist: Mindi Shapiro Levine
Assistant Photo Stylist: Mary Louise Menendez
Senior Production Manager: Sue Chodakiewicz
Senior Production Manager: Greg Amason

Contributors

Content Editor: Holley Johnson Grainger, M.S., R.D.
Recipe Developers and Testers: Erica Hopper, Tonya Johnson,
    Kyra Moncrief, Kathleen Royal Phillips
Copy Editors: Donna Baldone, Jasmine Hodges
Proofreaders: Rebecca Benton, *Marrathon* Production Services
Indexer: Mary Ann Laurens
Interns: Megan Branagh, Frances Gunnells, Susan Kemp,
    Sara Lyon, Staley McIlwain, Laura Medlin, Jeffrey Preis,
    Maria Sanders, Julia Sayers, April Smitherman
Food Stylist: Ana Kelly
Photographer: Becky Luigart-Stayner
Photo Stylist: Leslie Simpson

MyRecipes.com

General Manager, Time Inc. Lifestyle Digital: Tina Imm
Content Director: Jason Burnett
Senior Editor: Anne Chappell Cain, M.S., R.D.
Production Manager: Jim Sheetz
SEO Editor/Producer: Emily Shepherd
Associate Editor/Producer: Ashley Kappel
Assistant Editor/Producer: Erin McFarland
Production Assistant: Jessica Snead
Intern: Elizabeth Branch

Time Home Entertainment Inc.

Publisher: Jim Childs
Vice President, Brand & Digital Strategy: Steven Sandonato
Executive Director, Marketing Services: Carol Pittard
Executive Director, Retail & Special Sales: Tom Mifsud
Director, Bookazine Development & Marketing: Laura Adam
Executive Publishing Director: Joy Butts
Associate Publishing Director: Megan Pearlman
Finance Director: Glenn Buonocore
Associate General Counsel: Helen Wan

To order additional publications, call
1-800-765-6400 or 1-800-491-0551.

To search, savor, and share thousands of recipes,
visit MyRecipes.com.

COVER (from left to right, top to bottom): Melon Ball Salad with Lime Syrup, page 185; Caramelized Onion–and–Blue Cheese Mini Burgers, page 46; Summer Squash Ribbons with Lemon and Parmesan, page 177; Mozzarella, Tomato, and Basil Salad, page 179; Chili-Lime Drumsticks, page 28; Waldorf Spinach Salad, page 175; Luscious Lemon Bars, page 217; Bacon-Brown Sugar Brussels Sprouts, page 162; Cherry-Almond Crisp, page 227; Pork with Apples, Bacon, and Sauerkraut, page 66; Caramelized Spicy Green Beans, page 171; Loaded Twice-Baked Potatoes, page 207

BACK COVER (from left to right, top to bottom): Tart Lemon Ice with Crushed Strawberries, page 244; Chocolate-Caramel Pecan Pie, page 240; Everyday Roast Vegetables, page 181; Pork and Tomato Skillet Sauté, page 61; Grilled Corn Poblano Salad with Chipotle Vinaigrette, page 169; Real Banana Pudding, page 235; Broccoli Slaw with Candied Pecans, page 158; Grilled Baby Back Ribs with Sticky Brown Sugar Glaze, page 72; Rosemary-Garlic Chicken Quarters, page 29; Steamed Carrots with Garlic-Ginger Butter, page 163; Roasted Baby Beet Salad, page 157